HISTORIC
BUILDINGS *of*
MASSACHUSETTS

This catalog is based almost completely on a publication issued in 1965 by the Secretary of the Commonwealth, Kevin H. White, Chairman of the Massachusetts Historical Commission, which was made possible by a generous special appropriation by the General Court of Massachusetts in the Supplementary Budget for 1964–1965. In its publication, the Commission thanked Mr. James C. Massey, Supervisory Architect of the Eastern Office of the Historic American Buildings Survey, and Mr. John C. Poppeliers, Editor. Thanks were also given to Dr. Abbott Lowell Cummings, Assistant Director of the Society for the Preservation of New England Antiquities, and Mr. J. Peter Spang, III, of the Heritage Foundation, as well as to members of the Junior League of Boston, Inc.

HISTORIC BUILDINGS *of* MASSACHUSETTS

Photographs from the Historic American Buildings Survey

SCRIBNER
HISTORIC BUILDINGS
SERIES

CHARLES SCRIBNER'S SONS • NEW YORK

Copyright © 1976 Charles Scribner's Sons

Library of Congress Cataloging in Publication Data

Historic American Buildings Survey.
  Historic buildings of Massachusetts.

  (Scribner historic buildings series)
  1. Architecture—Massachusetts—Pictorial works.
2. Historic buildings—Massachusetts—Pictorial works.
I. Title.
NA730.M4H57 1976   779'.9'9744   76–12600
ISBN 0–684–14567–7
ISBN 0–684–14560–X pbk.

1 3 5 7 9 11 13 15 17 19 C/C 20 18 16 14 12 10 8 6 4 2
1 3 5 7 9 11 13 15 17 19 C/P 20 18 16 14 12 10 8 6 4 2

Printed in the United States of America

Contents

PREFACE

The Historic American Buildings Survey, organized in 1933 by the National Park Service in collaboration with the American Institute of Architects and Library of Congress, is a long-range program to assemble an archives of American architecture. During the 1930s thousands of valuable records were gathered throughout the United States and deposited at the Library of Congress. The program ceased at the start of World War II and was reinstituted in 1957.

In addition to the advice and co-operation of the American Institute of Architects and the National Trust for Historic Preservation, the Survey operates in close collaboration with universities, historical societies, preservation groups, and state and local government agencies. Administration is by the National Park Service, with the HABS recording directed by the Service's Division of Architecture in Design and Construction Offices in Philadelphia, Washington, and San Francisco. The Philadelphia office is responsible for work in the eastern half of the country (except the District of Columbia), including states on the western bank of the Mississippi River and the Caribbean. Inquiries may be addressed to the Survey's

Philadelphia office: Eastern Office of Design and Construction, National Park Service, 143 South Third Street, Philadelphia, Pennsylvania 19106.

Architectural interest and merit, as well as historical associations, are the basic criteria for the selection of buildings for the Survey. HABS has recorded a wide variety of building types, public and private, large and small, to insure a thorough record of our diverse architectural heritage. Priority has always been given to buildings threatened with demolition or alteration.

New methods of recording have been employed to extend the limited funds available to the Survey and to make records more useful to the architects, planners, historians, and restorationists who make wide use of the Survey. An emphasis on high-quality photographs, accompanied by thorough architectural and historical documentation, has expanded the range and depth of recording. Architectural photogrammetry has also been used to record buildings that are too large and complex to be economically measured by other means. Working with university architectural departments, the Survey has received many fine drawings made through student measured-drawing programs.

Since 1957, the HABS has been the recipient of many important gifts. Donations of measured drawings, photographs, and data are a new and significant phase of the work, and are especially welcome. Such gifts are federal income tax deductible.

The Historic American Buildings Survey's archives at the Library of Congress is one of the world's largest collections of architectural records, including measured drawings, photographs, and architectural and historical documentation, for 10,000 historic buildings throughout the United States, Puerto Rico, and the Virgin Islands. A detailed, geographically arranged *Catalog* was published in 1941 and a *Supplement* in 1959. New catalogs are being published by states because of the increasing size of the collection.

The recording program in Massachusetts was originally undertaken in 1934 under the direction of Frank Chouteau Brown, FAIA, and continued from 1939 until 1941 with Public Works funds. Over 410 structures were recorded in Massachusetts by 1941. Frank Chouteau Brown, working on the American Institute of Architects' Edward Langley Scholarship, completed over ninety sheets of measured drawings in Massachusetts for HABS in the early 1940s. Although the program was discontinued with the advent of World War II, many measured drawings were presented as gifts from institutions and individuals.

Recording in Massachusetts was resumed by the National Park Service at the Adams National Historic Site in Quincy in 1956, and state-wide in 1957. Several Massachusetts projects since that time have been undertaken by the Survey, including work on Cape Cod in 1960, 1961, and 1962; in the Connecticut River Valley, centered in Deerfield, in 1959; at Salem, centered on the Salem Maritime National Historic Site, in 1950; and in Lexington and Concord, centered in the Minute Man National Historical Park, in 1961 and 1962. Smaller projects have more recently been arranged in co-operation with Shaker Community, Inc. at Hancock; Shakerton Foundation, Inc. at Harvard; in New Bedford; and in Boston with the Society for the Preservation of New England Antiquities, and with the Boston Redevelopment Authority.

This book lists over 800 structures. This comprises updatings and revisions of structures included in the 1941 *Catalog* and the 1959 *Supplement*, as well as new recordings.

The format used for the listings is the abbreviated form used in the 1941 *HABS Catalog*, which includes: historic name of the structure; HABS number; address, when known; brief description; date of building, additions, and alterations; architect or builder, when known; and a listing of measured drawings, photographs, photocopies, and data pages that are available in the HABS archives. Following are abbreviations and symbols which have been used:

MASS-342– Historic American Buildings Survey number. All buildings recorded by the Survey are assigned an HABS number. These numbers should be used when inquiring about a structure or ordering reproductions.

sheets — sheets of measured drawings
n.d. — no date ascertainable
* — an asterisk after a date indicates that the measured drawings, photographs, or date pages made on that date are temporarily held in the HABS Philadelphia office.

For each building surveyed, one or more exterior photographs were taken. Sometimes these were supplemented by photographs of the interior too. Each listing in the catalog indicates how many photographs are available in the files of HABS. Reproducing every one of the HABS photographs for each of the buildings surveyed would have made too cumbersome a book. The most appealing and significant photographs were chosen for the great majority of the entries, although some had to be omitted because of lack of space or because the photographs were of poor quality; some of the newer work in Nantucket and New Bedford, where catalog entries have not yet been published, had to be omitted too. On the following few pages, all of the HABS photographs for one structure— the Captain William Wildes House in Weymouth (MASS-835)—are reproduced. Although this house was recorded in more detail than most of the other structures were, the photographs will give some idea of the comprehensive nature of the HABS Survey.

WEYMOUTH, MASSACHUSETTS
Captain William Wildes House

Wildes, Captain William, House (MASS–835), 872 Commercial St. Frame with clapboarding, 2 stories, hipped roof and monitor; built 1790. 5 ext. photos (1938), 8 int. photos (1938).

Historic American Buildings Survey

MASSACHUSETTS CATALOG

List of Measured Drawings,
Photographs, and Written Documentation

•

Compiled and Edited by
Historic American Buildings Survey
Eastern Office Design and Construction
National Park Service
Department of the Interior

•

John C. Poppeliers, *Editor*

ACOAXET (See WESTPORT)

ACTON — *Middlesex County*

Faulkner House (MASS-543), High St. Frame with clapboarding, two stories, rear and side wings; built late 17th or early 18th C., later additions. 5 ext. photos (1941).

ADAMS — *Berkshire County*

Society of Friends (Quaker) Meetinghouse (MASS-2-44), corner West Rd. and Maple St. Frame with clapboarding, two stories; built 1786. 4 sheets (1934); 1 ext. photo (1934).

AGAWAM — *Hampden County*

Colton-Cooley House (MASS-2-51), 740 Elm St. at Main. Frame with clapboarding and pilasters, 2 stories, hipped roof; built c. 1800. 8 sheets (1934); 2 ext. photos (1934).

Leonard, Captain Charles, House (MASS-2-50), 663 Main St. Frame with clapboarding, 2 stories, hipped roof; built 1805–07. 14 sheets (1934); 2 ext. photos (1934), 1 int. photo (1934).

Tobacco Barn (MASS-151), rear of 663 Main St. Frame with vertical siding, one story; built 1885. 1 sheet (1934); 1 photo (1937).

AMESBURY — Essex County

Powder House (MASS-338). Stucco, late 18th C. 1 ext. photo (1935).

1

Rocky Hill Meetinghouse (MASS-250), corner Elm St. and Portland Road. Frame with clapboarding, two stories with two-story entry wing; built 1785. 29 sheets (1937); 8 ext. photos (1937), 17 int. photos (1937).

AMHERST — *Hampshire County*

Boltwood-Stockbridge House (MASS-636), on University of Massachusetts campus, at N. edge of Amherst. Frame with clapboarding, two stories; built c. 1728, restored 1934–36. 3 ext. photos (1959), 1 int. photo (1959); 4 data pages (1959).

Strong, Nehemiah, House (MASS-650), 67 Amity St. Museum. Frame with clapboarding, 2 stories; built 1744. 3 ext. photos (1959), 2 int. photos (1959); 3 data pages (1959).

ANDOVER — *Essex County*

Abbot, Benjamin, Farmhouse (MASS-2-9), Andover St. and Argilla Road. Frame with clapboarding, two stories, rear lean-to, side barn wing; built late 17th or early 18th C. 12 sheets (1934); 3 ext. photos (1934), 1 int. photo (1934).

ANNISQUAM (See GLOUCESTER)

ARLINGTON — *Middlesex County*

Calvary Methodist Episcopal Church Tower (MASS-589), Massachusetts Ave. Cupola from Boylston Market, Boston; built 1809, market demolished 1888. Charles Bulfinch, architect. 1 ext. photo (1941).

Russell, Jason, House (MASS-588), 7 Jason St. Museum.

Frame with clapboarding, two stories; built c. 1740, later additions, moved from original site. Russell and eleven Minutemen died here in Battle of April 19, 1775. 1 ext. photo (1941).

ASHBY — *Middlesex County*

Fitch House (MASS-230), South Rd. See Kendall, Asa, House; Ashby, Mass.

Kendall, Asa, House ("John Fitch House") (MASS-230), South Road. Brick, two-and-a-half stories, hipped roof with side shed roofs; built c. 1790 on site of John Fitch House. 9 sheets (1936, 1937); 1 ext. photo (1936).

ASHFIELD — *Franklin County*

Congregational Meetinghouse (MASS-436). See Town Hall; Ashfield, Mass.

St. John's Episcopal Church (MASS-648), SW. corner Main St. and Baptist Corner Rd. Frame with clapboarding, one story with gallery, square tower; built 1824–27. Jonathan Lilly, master builder. 3 ext. photos (1959), 2 int. photos (1959); 3 data pages (1959).

Town Hall (MASS-436, MASS-651), S. side of Main St., near village center. Frame with clapboarding, two stories with tower; built 1812–14 as Congregational Meetinghouse. 3 ext. photos (1959), 1 int. photo (1959); 4 data pages (1959).

ASHLAND — *Middlesex County*

Frankland, Sir Henry, Garden (MASS-202), Old Bay Path. Three-terrace garden; laid out 1752, destroyed. 1 sheet (1936).

ATHOL — *Worcester County*

Old Meetinghouse (MASS-893). Frame with clapboarding, two stories with three-stage tower; built 1827. 2 ext. photos (1930's).

ATTLEBORO — *Bristol County*

Robinson, Joel, House (MASS-437). Frame with clapboarding, 2 stories; built late 18th C. 1 ext. photo (1935).

Thatcher House (MASS-339). Frame with clapboarding, 2 stories; built early 19th C. 3 ext. photos (1938), 1 int. photo (1935).

Well Sweep (MASS-438). 1 photo (1938).

ATTLEBORO VICINITY

Daggett, John, House (MASS-174), 480 N. Main St. Frame with clapboarding, two stories; built 1797. 6 sheets (1935); 2 ext. photos (1937).

AUBURN — *Worcester County*

Chapin, Thaddeus, House (MASS-340). Frame with clapboarding, two stories, hipped roof, rear and side wings; built late 18th C., later additions and alterations. 2 ext. photos (1936).

AUBURNDALE (See NEWTON)

BARNSTABLE — *Barnstable County*

Crocker, Cornelius, Tavern (MASS-694), S. side Main St. (State Rt. 6A). Frame with clapboarding and shin-

4

gles, two-and-a-half stories; built c. 1754. 6 sheets (1962*); 3 photocopies of prerestoration drawings (n.d.*); 4 data pages (1962*).

Gorham, Isaac, House (MASS-425). Wood, 2 stories; built mid 18th C. 2 ext. photos (1936), 3 int. photos (1936).

West Parish Congregational Meetinghouse (MASS-779), just off U.S. Rt. 6, at State Rt. 149, W. Barnstable. Frame with clapboarding, 2 stories with square bell tower; built 1717, enlarged and restored. 1 ext. photo (1959*); 4 data pages (1959*).

BEDFORD — *Middlesex County*

First Parish Unitarian Meetinghouse (MASS-538). Frame with clapboarding, two stories with square tower and cupola; built c. 1817. 4 ext. photos (1941).

Penniman-Stearns House (MASS-592), N. side State Rt. 62. Frame with clapboarding, two stories, hipped roof, side and rear wings; built 1796. Reuben Durin, architect. 5 ext. photos (1941).

Pollard Tavern (MASS-142), Great Rd. Frame with clapboarding, two-and-a-half stories, rear ell; built 1740, ruinous. 10 sheets (1934); 2 ext. photos (1937).

BEDFORD VICINITY

Garrison House (MASS-539), at Bedford Springs. Frame with clapboarding and shingles, two stories, rear lean-to; built 1664, later additions. 1 ext. photo (1941).

BEVERLY — *Essex County*

Balch, John, House (MASS-584), 448 Cabot St. Frame with clapboarding and shingles, two stories; nucleus dates from 1638, early additions. 2 ext. photos (1941).

Cabot, John, House and Garden (MASS-282), 117 Cabot St. Brick, three stories, hipped roof with balustrade; small garden with wooden gazebo; built and laid out 1781. 5 sheets (1938); 3 ext. photos (1940).

First Baptist Church Pulpit (MASS-619). Low, three-sided, paneled wooden pulpit; built c. 1802. 1 sheet (1944).

Foster, George B., House and Fence (MASS-267), 21 Bartlett St. Frame house with clapboarding, three stories; built c. 1788, fence 1870. 1 sheet (1938); 3 ext. photos (1940).

Foster Warehouse (MASS-260). Brick, three stories; built early 19th C. 3 ext. photos (1940).

Kilham, Austin D., House Garden (MASS-266), 8 Thorndike St. Formal garden with wooden fences, pergola; laid out 1844. 4 sheets (1938); 2 photos (1940).

Pierce, Benjamin, House (MASS-606), 305 Cabot St. Frame with clapboarding, 3 stories, hipped roof; built 1802, demolished 1942. 12 sheets (1941–42).

Powder House (MASS-583), Powder House Hill. Brick, one story, hexagonal; built early 19th C. Built for War of 1812. 1 ext. photo (1941).

Second Church (MASS-585). Frame with clapboarding,

one story with square tower, pilasters; built early 19th C. 1 ext. photo (1941).

BILLERICA — *Middlesex County*

Allen Tavern (MASS-528). Frame with clapboarding and shingles, two-and-a-half stories; built late 18th–early 19th C., several additions and alterations. 1 ext. photo (1941).

Bowers, Dr. William, House (MASS-530). Frame with clapboarding and brick end walls, two-and-a-half stories, monitor roof; built early 19th C. 2 ext. photos (1941).

First Parish Unitarian Church (MASS-529). Frame with clapboarding & matched siding, two stories, Doric portico, three-stage tower; built early 19th C. 2 ext. photos (1941).

Little Red School House (MASS-591). Frame with clapboarding, one story, pyramidal roof; built 19th C., ruinous. 1 photo (1941).

Locke, Honorable Joseph, House (MASS-531). Frame with clapboarding, two stories, pyramidal roof; built early 19th C. 1 ext. photo (1941).

BILLERICA VICINITY

Manning, Ensign Samuel, Manse (MASS-532), Chelmsford Road, .4 miles West of Rt. 3A. Frame with clapboarding, 2 stories, rear lean-to; built 1696, later additions. 2 ext. photos (1941).

BLACKSTONE — *Worcester County*

Old Stone Building (MASS-459). Fieldstone and stucco, three-and-a-half stories; built early 19th C., altered. 2 ext. photos (1941).

BOSTON — *Suffolk County*

Abolition Church (MASS-2-74), Smith Court. Brick, three stories; built 1806 for a black congregation. 3 sheets (1934); 3 ext. photos (1935, 1937), 7 int. photos (1935, 1937).

Adams, Major, House (MASS-352), Charlestown. Frame with clapboarding, three stories, side wings; built mid 18th C., later alterations, demolished 1964. 3 ext. photos (1936, 1941), 2 int. photos (1936).

Amory-Ticknor House (MASS-175), 9 Park St. at Beacon. Brick, four stories; built 1804, additions and alterations 1885. Charles Bulfinch, architect. 18 sheets (1936); 5 ext. photos (1934, 1935); 2 photocopies of ext. photos (c. 1885), 6 photocopies of int. photos (c. 1885).

Andrews-Getchell House (MASS-191), 21 Cordis Ave., Charlestown. Brick with frame ell, 3 stories, hipped roof; built c. 1820. 16 sheets (1935); 2 ext. photos (1935), 2 int. photos (1935).

Appleton, Nathan, House (Women's City Club) (MASS-813), 40 Beacon St. Brick, four-and-a-half stories, three-bay front with bow; built c. 1818, fourth-floor addition 1888. Attributed to Alexander Parris, architect; 1888 addition by H. W. Hartwell and W. S. Richardson. 2 sheets (1962*, details of Rumford Roaster); 2 int. photos

(1962*, Roaster details); 3 data pages (1960's*, including twin house at 39 Beacon St.).

Arlington Street Church (Unitarian) (MASS-817), NW. corner Boylston and Arlington Sts. Brownstone, 2 stories with front tower and steeple; built 1859–61. Arthur D. Gilman and Gridley J. F. Bryant, architects. One of the earliest examples of 18th C. revival style. 2 ext. photos (1961*), 5 int. photos (1961*).

Bird-Sawyer House (MASS-278), 41 Humphreys St., Dorchester. Frame with clapboarding, 2 stories, rear lean-to; built c. 1637, additions and alterations 1667, 1776, demolished c. 1950. 12 sheets (1939, 1940); 4 ext. photos (1940), 6 int. photos (1940), 1 photocopy of photo (1905), 3 photocopies of sketches showing house as it appeared 1637, 1667, 1776.

Blake, James, House (MASS-560), 735 Columbia Road, Dorchester. Museum. Frame with shingles, 2 stories, casement windows; mid 17th C., moved from original site. 2 ext. photos (1941, 1963*), 6 int. photos (1963*); 2 data pages (1963*).

Boston City Hall (MASS-860), N. side School St. Granite ashlar and brick, four-and-a-half stories with tower, Second Empire style; built 1862–65. Gridley J. F. Bryant and Arthur D. Gilman, architects. 4 ext. photos (1961*, 1962*), 10 int. photos (1961*), 8 photocopies of plans, elevations, and photographs (c. 1865*); 5 data pages (1962*).

Building (MASS-788), 15 Elm Street. Frame with clapboarding, three and four stories; probably built late 18th C., numerous alterations, demolished 1962. 1 ext. photo (1962*); 3 data pages (1964*).

9

Butler School (MASS-564), River St. Hyde Park. Frame with clapboarding and matched siding and pilasters, one story; built 1804. 1 ext. photo (1941).

Christ Church ("Old North Church") (MASS-500), 193 Salem St. Brick, two stories with three-stage square tower and spire; built 1723, spire replaced 1804 and 1954, restored 1912–14. William Price, architect. 2 ext. photos (1941).

Clap, Bela and Caleb, Houses (MASS-2-80), 44–46 Temple St. Frame with clapboarding, three stories, double house; built 1787, demolished. 10 sheets (1934); 1 ext. photo (1935), 3 int. photos (1935).

Clap, Roger, House (MASS-190), 199 Boston Street, Dorchester. Frame with clapboarding and shingles, two stories, gambrel roof; built 18th C., additions 1767, moved from Willow Ct. 1940's. 30 sheets (1935).

Clough, Ebenezer, House (MASS-342, 342A), 21 Unity St. See Clough-Langdon House; Boston, Mass.

Clough-Langdon House (MASS-342, 342A), 21 Unity St. Brick, three stories; built c. 1715, additions and alterations c. 1800, c. 1870 (1872 ell now removed). 8 sheets (1927, 1943); 5 ext. photos (1936, 1959), 7 int. photos (1959); 4 data pages (1960, 1961).

Codman Building (MASS-784), 30–48 Hanover St. Brick with brownstone front, five stories, two projecting bays; built c. 1859, demolished 1963. 2 ext. photos (1962*); 2 data pages (1963*).

Curtis House (MASS-479), Roxbury. Frame with clapboarding and shingles, brick, two stories; built early

19th C., later additions and alterations, demolished 1940. 2 ext. photos (1940), 2 int. photos (1940).

Devens, General Charles, House (MASS-346), 30 Union St., Charlestown. Frame with clapboarding, brick end walls, three-and-a-half stories, rear ell; built early 19th C., later alterations. 2 ext. photos (1936).

Dillaway-Thomas House (MASS-558), Eliot Square, Roxbury. Museum. Frame with clapboarding, two-and-a-half stories, gambrel roof; nucleus built 1714, additions and alterations mid 18th C. and early 19th C. 2 ext. photos (1941).

Everett, Edward, House (MASS-347), 16 Harvard St., Charlestown. Brick, 3 stories; built 1812, Ionic porch later addition. 2 ext. photos (1936), 3 int. photos (1936).

Faneuil Hall (MASS-163), Dock Sq. Brick, three stories with tower and cupola; built 1742, rebuilt after fire 1763, enlarged 1806. John Lambert Smibert (1742), Charles Bulfinch (1806), architects. Referred to as the "Cradle of Liberty." 3 sheets (1935, committee and commandery rooms); 6 int. photos (1937, commandery room).

First Church in Roxbury (MASS-557), Eliot Square, Roxbury. Frame with clapboarding and matched siding, two stories, four-stage tower with cupola; built 1804. 4 ext. photos (1941).

First Parish Unitarian Church (MASS-569), Church and Parish Sts., Dorchester. Frame with clapboarding and pilasters, two stories, four-stage tower and cupola; built 1743, enlarged 1795. 2 ext. photos (1941).

Fort Independence (MASS-570), Castle Island. Coursed ashlar; built 1801, not used after 1880. 6 ext. photos (1941).

Fort Winthrop–Citadel (MASS-617), Governor's Island. Stone and brick; citadel with courtyard, bastions and moat; built 1852, demolished 1946. 13 sheets (1946).

Franklin Place and Tontine Crescent (MASS-612), Franklin St. between Hawley and Devonshire Sts. Brick, three stories; built 1795, demolished 1858. Charles Bulfinch, architect. 1 sheet (1943–44, plans with elevations of Tontine central pavilion and Boston Theater).

"The Gothic" Apartment House (MASS-669), 47 Allen St. Stone and brick, five stories; built c. 1900, demolished 1960. 2 ext. photos (1959), 2 int. photos (1959); 2 data pages (1960, 1961).

Hale, Edward Everett, House (MASS-559), 39 Highland, Roxbury. Frame with clapboarding and matched siding, two-and-a-half stories, giant tetrastyle Ionic portico; built mid 19th C. 1 ext. photo (1941).

Hayden, Judge, House and Garden (MASS-294), 281 Heath St., Roxbury. Frame with clapboarding, two stories, giant tetrastyle Ionic portico; built early 19th C., garden laid out c. 1856. Demolished by 1965. 1 sheet (1938–39); 2 ext. photos (1940), 1 int. photo (1940).

Hollis Street Church (MASS-156), Hollis St. Brick, two stories with square tower and spire; built 1810, altered 1885 for theater (see Hollis Street Theater, MASS-157), demolished 1935. 5 sheets (1935); 4 photocopies of photos (c. 1860, c. 1870, 2 ext., 2 int.).

12

Hollis Street Theater (MASS-157), Hollis St. Brick, 2 and 3 stories; Hollis Street Church remodeled 1885 into theater, demolished 1935. John R. Hall, architect for remodeling. 6 sheets (1935); 2 ext. photos (1935), 6 int. photos (1935).

House (William Clapp) (MASS-447), 195 Boston St., Dorchester. Frame with clapboarding, brick end wall, two-and-a-half stories with two-story wing; built 1806, later additions. 2 ext. photos (1937).

House (MASS-348), 11 Devens Street, Charlestown. Frame with clapboarding, two-and-a-half stories and two-story wing, gambrel roof; built mid 18th C., later additions, demolished. 3 ext. photos (1935), 3 int. photos (1935).

House (MASS-671), 91 Green St. at Leverett. Frame, three stories; built c. 1810, demolished 1960. 1 ext. photo (1959), 4 int. photos (1959); 2 data pages (1960).

House (MASS-670), 47 McLean St. Brick row house, four-and-a-half stories; built second quarter 19th C., demolished 1960. 3 ext. photos (1959), 4 int. photos (1959); 3 data pages (1959).

Houses (MASS-790), corner Scollay Square (1–11) and Cornhill (83–91). Brick, three and three-and-a-half stories, hipped and mansard roofs; built c. 1817, later additions and alterations, demolished 1960's. 5 ext. photos (1962*).

Hyde, George, House (MASS-192), 69 Rutherford Avenue, Charlestown. Frame with clapboarding, two-and-a-half stories, gambrel roof; built c. 1800, demolished by

1965. 7 sheets (1935); 4 ext. photos (1935), 3 int. photos (1935).

Hyde-Lincoln House (MASS-299), 32 Cordis St., Charlestown. Frame with clapboarding, 3 stories with two-story side wing; built 1801. 10 sheets (1940, 1941); 4 ext. photos (1941), 3 int. photos (1941).

Hyde-Worthen House (MASS-192). See Hyde, George, House (MASS-192); Boston, Mass.

India Wharf Stores (MASS-2-76), 306–08 Atlantic Ave. Brick, five and six stories; built 1808, partially destroyed 1868, demolished 1962. Charles Bulfinch, architect. Five sheets (1934); 4 ext. photos (1935), 3 photocopies of photos (before 1868).

Iron Standard and Gate (MASS-2-11). Tremont Place. Cast iron. 1 sheet (1934); 2 photos (1934).

Loring-Greenough House and Garden (MASS-272), 12 South St., Jamaica Plain. Frame with clapboarding, two-and-a-half stories; central path garden; built and laid out c. 1758, later alterations. 2 sheets (1937, 1938); 2 ext. photos (1940).

Lyceum Hall (MASS-571), Meetinghouse Hill, Dorchester. Frame with clapboarding and matched siding, two stories, giant tetrastyle Ionic portico; built mid 19th C., alterations. 1 ext. photo (1941).

Marshall-Hancock House (MASS-2-55, 2-55A), 10 Marshall St. at Creek Square. Brick, three stories; built c. 1760, additions late 18th C. 7 sheets (1934, 1943); 1 ext. photo (1934), 2 int. photos (1934).

14

Massachusetts Charitable Mechanic Association Exhibition Hall (MASS-672), Huntington Ave. and W. Newton St. Brick with brownstone and terra cotta trim, three stories with tower; built 1881, demolished 1959. William G. Preston, architect. 4 ext. photos (1959), 1 int. photo (1957), 1 photocopy late 19th C. print; 4 data pages (1960, 1962).

Massachusetts General Hospital Bulfinch Building (MASS-556), Fruit St. Coursed ashlar, 2 stories on rusticated basement, hipped roof, giant hexastyle Ionic portico; built 1818. Charles Bulfinch, architect. 3 ext. photos (1941).

Massachusetts Institute of Technology Rogers Building (MASS-252), 491 Boylston St. Brick with stone trim, four stories on high granite basement, giant tetrastyle Corinthian portico; built 1865, demolished 1939. William G. Preston, architect. 23 sheets (1938, 1939); 6 ext. photos (1939), 9 int. photos (1939).

Mayhew School (MASS-673), Poplar and Chambers Streets. Brick with Gothic ornamentation, three-and-a-half stories; built 1897, demolished 1960. Design possibly by Stanford White. 4 ext. photos (1959), 4 int. photos (1959); 2 data pages (1960).

"Old North Church" (MASS-500). See Christ Church (MASS-500); Boston, Mass.

"Old Puddingstone" Building (MASS-126), 199 Ruggles Street, Roxbury. Random-coursed ashlar, one story; built c. 1825, demolished by 1965. 1 sheet (1934); 3 ext. photos (1935).

"Old West Church" (MASS-279), 131 Cambridge St.

15

Brick, two stories, three-and-a-half story projecting front with tower and cupola; built 1806, restored 1963. Asher Benjamin, architect. 4 ext. photos (1940*), 9 int. photos (1940*), 4 photocopies of old photos (n.d.*).

Otis, Harrison Gray, House (First) (MASS-845), 141 Cambridge Street. Historic house, museum and head-quarters of the Society for the Preservation of New England Antiquities. Brick, three-and-a-half stories; built 1796–97, later alterations. Attributed to Charles Bulfinch, architect. 5 ext. photos (1930's*), 1 int. photo (1930's*).

"Painters' Arms" (MASS-128), Hanover Street. Wooden guild sign with Latin motto; dated 1701. 1 photocopy of old photo (n.d.).

Park Street Church (Congregational) (MASS-631), corner Tremont and Park Sts. Brick, two stories with tower and spire; built 1809. Peter Banner and Solomon Willard, architects. 1 photocopy of old painting before alterations (n.d.).

Parker, Daniel P., House (Women's City Club) (MASS-814), 39 Beacon St. Brick, four-and-a-half stories, three-bay front including bow; built c. 1818, fourth-floor addition 1888. Attributed to Alexander Parris, archi-tect; 1888 addition by H. W. Hartwell and W. S. Richardson. 7 int. photos (1940*); 3 data pages (1960's*, including twin house at 40 Beacon St.).

Parkman Market (MASS-2-47), corner Cambridge and N. Grove Sts. Brick, three stories, cupola; built 1810, partially destroyed 1924, by 1960 demolished. 6 sheets (1934); 2 ext. photos (1934).

16

Pierce, Moses, House (Hichborn House) (MASS-499), 29 North Sq. Brick, three stories, two-bay front; built c. 1711, extensively altered. 2 ext. photos (1941).

Pierce, Robert, House (MASS-562), Oakton Ave., Neponset Village, Dorchester. Frame with clapboarding, two stories, rear lean-to; built 1640, early additions. 1 photocopy of old photo (n.d.).

Pierce, Thomas, House (MASS-561), corner Adams and Minot Sts., Dorchester. Frame with clapboarding, one-and-a-half stories, gambrel roof, rear wing; built before 1795, later additions and alterations. 1 ext. photo (1941).

The Province House (MASS-816). See Sergeant, Peter, House (MASS-816); Boston, Mass.

Reed, Reuben, Building (MASS-785), 7–9 Elm St. Brick with granite-faced front, five stories; built c. 1842, later additions, demolished 1962. 3 ext. photos (1962*); 3 data pages (1964*).

Revere, Paul, House (MASS-491), 19 North Square. Museum. Frame with clapboarding, two stories with overhang; built c. 1677, third-floor addition and extensive alterations mid and late 18th C., restored 1908 to 17th C. appearance. Owned by the noted patriot from 1770 to 1800. 1 ext. photo (1941).

St. Augustine's Chapel and Cemetery (MASS-2-26), Dorchester and West Sixth Sts., South Boston. Brick, one story, apse and shed wing; chapel built 1818, enlarged 1833. 6 sheets (1934); 1 ext. photo (1934).

St. Patrick's Church (MASS-154), Northampton St.

Brick with frame apse, 2 stories with square tower; built 1836. 11 sheets (1935); 1 ext. photo (1935).

"Savage House" (MASS-503), 30 Dock Square. Brick, three stories; built early 18th C., destroyed 1926. 2 sheets (c. 1920).

Sears' Block (MASS-786), 72 Cornhill at Court St. Frame and brick with granite facing, partially built 1816, extensively rebuilt 1839–50's, alterations 1870's. 2 ext. photos (1962*), 1 int. photo (1962*).

Sears' Convex Block (Sears' Crescent) (MASS-787), 50–56 Cornhill. Brick, five and six stories, six-bay center with flanking wings; partially built 1816, extensively altered, rebuilt and enlarged 1854, later additions and alterations. 4 ext. photos (1962*); 3 data pages (1964*).

Second Church in Dorchester (MASS-563), corner Washington and Centre Sts., Dorchester. Frame with clapboarding and matched siding, two stories, three-stage tower and cupola; built 1808. 3 ext. photos (1941).

Sergeant, Peter, House (The Province House) (MASS-816), Washington St. opposite Milk St. Brick, four stories, built 1676–79, remodeled 1728, walls incorporated in later business building, demolished 1922. 1 photocopy of photo of brickwork (1922).

Shirley-Eustis House (MASS-275), 31 Shirley St., Roxbury. Frame with clapboarding, two-and-a-half stories on high basement, pilasters and elaborate cornice, cupola; built 1746–48, alterations 1819, moved 70' in 1867. Residence of Govs. Shirley and Eustis. 14 sheets (1930's); 9 ext. photos (1939*, 1963*), 14 int. photos

(1939*, 1963*), 1 photocopy of old watercolor (n.d.*); 1 data page (1964*).

State House Gates and Steps (MASS-245), Beacon St. Granite and cast iron; built c. 1833. Alexander Parris and Solomon Willard, architects. 10 sheets (1938); 6 photos (1941).

Steps and Wrought-Iron Archway (MASS-2-11), Province & Bosworth Sts. Built 19th C. 1 sheet (1934); 2 photos (1934).

Third Baptist Society Church (MASS-544), Charles St. Brick, two stories with tower; built 1807, Asher Benjamin, architect. 1 ext. photo (1941).

Toolhouse (MASS-498), Copp's Hill Burial Ground. Frame with carved wooden panels; built mid 19th C. 4 ext. photos (1941).

Union Oyster House (Capen House) (MASS-127), 41–43 Union St. Brick, three-and-a-half stories, gambrel roof; built 1726. 3 sheets (1934); 1 ext. photo (1935).

United States Custom House (MASS-789), S. side State Street between India Street and McKinley Square. Ashlar, originally two stories with dome, giant Doric peristyle and portocoes; built 1847, 500-foot office tower added 1915. Ammi B. Young, architect (1847); Peabody and Stearns (1915). 1 photocopy of print (before 1860*).

United States Frigate *Constitution*, **Commodore's Quarters** (MASS-2-84), U.S. Navy Yard, Charlestown. Launched 1797. Joshua Humphreys, designer. 2 sheets (1934); 3 int. photos (1934).

United States Navy Yard Commandant's House (MASS-2-10), United States Navy Yard, Chelsea Street, Charlestown. Brick, two-and-a-half stories, bowed rear bays; built 1809. 7 sheets (1934); 2 ext. photos (1934).

Warehouse (MASS-125), 68 Broad St. Brick, four stories, hipped roof; built 1806, altered 1934. 3 sheets (1934); 1 ext. photo (1935).

Women's City Club (MASS-813, 814), 39 and 40 Beacon St. See Appleton, Nathan, House (MASS-813), and Parker, Daniel P., House (MASS-814); Boston, Mass.

BOSTON AND BOSTON VICINITY

Mile Stones (MASS-128). Erected from early 18th to early 19th C. in Bristol, Essex, Norfolk, Middlesex, Suffolk, and Worcester Counties. 28 sheets (1935, 1936); 77 photos (1940).

BOXFORD — *Essex County*

Goodridge, Benjamin, House (MASS-2-30), about 1/4 mi. N. of Town Hall on road to Georgetown. Frame with clapboarding, 2 stories, rear lean-to; built 1740, destroyed by fire c. 1957. 10 sheets (1934, title "Daniel Gould House"); 1 ext. photo (1934).

Goodridge, Benjamin, Shoemaker's Shop (MASS-2-58), on the road to Georgetown. Frame with clapboarding, one story; built 1740. 1 sheet (1934); 1 ext. photo (1934).

Saw, Grist, and Knife Mill Group (MASS-2-15), 1/2 mi. S. of Town Hall on road to Middleton. Frame with matched siding and shingles, 1 story; built 1710. 5 sheets (1934); 4 ext. photos (1934), 2 int. photos (1934).

BREWSTER — *Barnstable County*

Cobb, Captain Elijah, House (MASS-732), Lower Rd. Frame with clapboarding, two stories; built 1799. 1 ext. photo (1959*); 4 data pages (1959*).

Dillingham, Isaac, House (MASS-733), State Rt. 6A. Frame with shingles, two stories, "salt-box" type. 2 ext. photos (1959*); 1 data page (1959*).

House (MASS-439), Brewster Mill. 3 int. photos (1936).

Stony Brook Mill (MASS-179), Old Coach Rd. Frame with shingles, two stories; built 1872, reconstructed 1940. 3 sheets (1936); 3 ext. photos (1935, 1959*); 1 data page (1959*).

Winslow House (MASS-344). Frame with clapboarding, 2 stories; built mid 18th C. 2 ext. photos (1936), 3 int. photos (1936).

BRIDGEWATER — *Plymouth County*

Andrews House (MASS-2-91), 38 Walnut St. See Pratt, Betty, House (MASS-2-91); Bridgewater, Mass.

Hayward House (MASS-343). Frame with clapboarding and shingles, two stories, rear lean-to; built early 19th C. 1 ext. photo (1937), 1 photocopy of old ext. photo (n.d.).

Pratt, Betty, House (Andrews House) (MASS-2-91), 38 Walnut St. Frame with shingles, two stories, rear lean-to and wing; built c. 1780. 5 sheets (1934); 4 ext. photos (1935), 3 int. photos (1935).

BRIMFIELD — *Hampden County*

Chamberlain House (MASS-311). Frame with clapboarding and matched siding, two stories, pedimented giant tetrastyle portico, rear wing; built early 19th C., later additions and alterations. 2 ext. photos (1930's*), 2 photocopies of old ext. photos (n.d.).

BROOKFIELD — *Worcester County*

Banister House (MASS-345). Frame with clapboarding, two stories, hipped roof; built mid 18th C. 4 ext. photos (1936), 8 int. photos (1936).

Crosby, Colonel J., House (MASS-133), Main St. Frame with clapboarding, two stories, rear wing; built 1797. 12 sheets (1934); 5 ext. photos (1935), 3 int. photos (1935).

BUCKLAND — *Franklin County*

Griswold, Major Joseph, House (Mary Lyon House) (MASS-108), Upper St., Buckland Center. Brick, two-and-a-half stories; built 1818. 7 sheets (1934, 1935); 3 ext. photos (1935), 1 int. photo (1935).

Lyon, Mary, House. (See Griswold, Major Joseph, House) (MASS-108); Buckland, Mass.

BURLINGTON — *Middlesex County*

Winn, William H., House (MASS-199), corner New Bridge Ave. and Winn St. Frame with clapboarding, two-and-a-half stories, hip-gambrel roof, rear ell; built 1732, demolished 1938. 10 sheets (1936); 5 ext. photos (1935), 2 int. photos (1935).

22

Wyman, Francis, House (MASS-298), Francis Wyman Rd. Frame with clapboarding, 2 stories; built 1666. 11 sheets (1941); 1 ext. photo (1936), 4 int. photos (1936).

CAMBRIDGE — *Middlesex County*

Apartment House (MASS-879), 1667 Cambridge St. Frame with clapboarding, three stories, front and rear porches, flat roof; built 1898. George Fogerthy, architect. Typical "three-decker" Boston area apartment house. 5 ext. photos (1964*), 2 int. photos (1964*); 2 data pages (1964*).

Batchelder, Francis, House (MASS-884), 467 Cambridge Street. Frame with clapboarding, two-and-a-half stories, gable roof; built 1825. 2 ext. photos (1964*), 4 int. photos (1964*); 2 data pages (1964*).

Bates, Moses, House (MASS-876), 69 Thorndike St. Frame with clapboarding, two-and-a-half stories, gable roof, ell, Ionic porch; built 1844. 2 ext. photos (1964*), 1 int. photo (1964*); 3 data pages (1964*).

Brattle, General William, House (MASS-274), 42 Brattle St. Frame with clapboarding, two-and-a-half stories, hipped roof, rear wing; built c. 1735. 3 ext. photos (1937), 5 int. photos (1937).

Christ Church (MASS-2-3), Garden St. Frame with horizontal siding, one story with square entry tower; built 1761, enlarged 1857. Peter Harrison, architect. 8 sheets (1934); 2 ext. photos (1934), 2 int. photos (1934).

Deane, Ezra, House (MASS-864), 23 Fayette St. Stuccoed brick, two-and-a-half stories, low hipped roof with wide bracketed cornice, cast iron grillwork on entrance porch and balconies; built 1848. 2 ext. photos (1964*), 3 int. photos (1964*); 3 data pages (1964*).

"The Dunster" (Harvard University, Dudley Hall) (MASS-818), E. side Dunster St., S. of Massachusetts Ave. Brick with limestone trim, five stories, Italian Renaissance palazzo style; built 1895–97, demolished 1964. Little, Browne, and Moore, architects. 2 int. photos (1964*), 1 photocopy of ink sketch (1896*); 10 data pages (1964*).

Fort Washington (MASS-2-48), Waverly St. Earthenwork; built 1775, restored 1857, 1900. Built by Continental Army under Washington. 3 sheets (1934); 2 ext. photos (1934).

Harvard University, Dudley Hall (MASS-818). See "The Dunster" (MASS-818); Cambridge, Mass.

Harvard University, Holden Chapel (MASS-2-1), Harvard College Yard. Brick, one story, pilasters; built 1744. 5 sheets (1934), 2 ext. photos (1934).

Harvard University, Hollis Hall (MASS-2-2), Harvard College. Brick, four stories, hipped roof; built 1763. Thomas Dawes, master builder. 10 sheets (1934); 3 ext. photos (1934).

Higginson, Stephen Jr., House (MASS-840), 7 Kirkland St. Frame with clapboarding, two-and-a-half stories, rear and side wings, gable roof; built c. 1819, later additions, demolished 1963. 2 ext. photos (1963*), 3 int. photos (1963*). Gift of James F. and Jean B. O'Gorman.

Houghton, Amory, House (MASS-865), 61 Otis St. Brick, three-and-a-half stories, party-wall house, gable roof, cast-iron balcony; built 1851. 1 ext. photo (1964*), 2 int. photos (1964*); 3 data pages (1964*).

House (MASS-782), 22 Appian Way. Frame with clapboarding, two-and-a-half stories; built 1820's, later additions, demolished 1963–64. 1 ext. photo (1963*).

Hoyt, Benjamin, House (MASS-866), 134 Otis St. Frame with clapboarding, two stories, gable roof, ell; built 1868. 2 int. photos (1964*); 2 data pages (1964*).

Hyatt, Alpheus, House (MASS-883), 19 Francis Ave. Frame with clapboarding, two-and-a-half stories, intersecting gambrel roofs, Queen Anne Style balustraded entrance porch, rear ell; built 1889. 4 ext. photos (1964*), 2 int. photos (1964*); 3 data pages (1889).

Ireland, Abraham, Gravestone (MASS-128), corner Massachusetts Ave. and Garden Street. Headstone; date 1753. 1 photo (1940).

Longfellow House (MASS-169), 105 Brattle St. See Vassall-Craigie-Longfellow House and Garden (MASS-169); Cambridge, Mass.

Middlesex County Jailer's House (MASS-873), 50 Thorndike St. Brick, two-and-a-half stories, mansard roof, projecting entrance bay; built 1872. 2 ext. photos (1964*); 3 data pages (1964*).

Middlesex County Registry of Deeds (MASS-877), Third and Cambridge Sts. Brick, four stories, flat roof, raised Ionic portico; built 1896. Olin W. Cutter, architect. 5 ext. photos (1964*); 2 data pages (1964*).

Norton-Johnson House (MASS-886), 85 Brattle St.

Frame with matched siding, 2 stories, gable roof; built 1848. 3 ext. photos (1964*), 1 int. photo (1964*); 2 data pages (1964*).

Saunders, Charles, House (MASS-870), 1627 Massachusetts Avenue. Frame with clapboarding, two-and-a-half stories, mansard roof, rear ell, balustraded front porch, cast-iron fence; built 1862. 6 ext. photos (1964*), 2 int. photos (1964*); 3 data pages (1964*).

Sewall, Stephen, House (MASS-618), 13 DeWolfe St. Frame with clapboarding, three stories; built 1765 at Harvard Yard, facing S. to Massachusetts Ave., moved and altered 1857. 2 sheets (1945).

Stevens-Hovey House (MASS-885), 75 Winter St. Frame with asbestos siding, two-and-a-half stories, gable roof, rear ell; built 1838. 2 ext. photos (1964*), 2 int. photos (1964*); 2 data pages (1964*).

Thorpe, Annie Longfellow, House (MASS-875), 115 Brattle St. Frame with clapboarding, two-and-a-half stories, gambrel roof, early Colonial Revival house; built 1887. Ernest W. Longfellow, architect. 4 ext. photos (1964*), 3 int. photos (1964*); 3 data pages (1964*).

Treadwell-Sparks House (MASS-869), 48 Quincy St. Frame with matched siding, two stories, hipped roof, side ell; built 1838. Home of Jared Sparks, president of Harvard College. 3 int. photos (1964*); 3 data pages (1964*).

Valentine-Fuller House and Garden (MASS-283A), 125 Prospect Street. Coursed ashlar, two stories, monitor; built mid 19th C., demolished 1937; garden laid out 1850. 1 sheet (1937–38); 2 photocopies of old photos (c. 1900).

Van Brunt, Henry, House (MASS-874), 167 Brattle St. Frame with clapboarding and shingles, two-and-a-half stories, gable roof; built 1883. Henry Van Brunt, architect. Home of a leading architect of his period. 2 ext. photos (1964*), 2 int. photos (1964*); 3 data pages (1964*).

Vassall-Craigie-Longfellow House and Garden (MASS-169), 105 Brattle St. Frame with clapboarding, two-and-a-half stories, Ionic pilasters & deck balustrade; built 1759, later additions. Part of Tory Row used as headquarters by Washington, and later the home of Henry Wadsworth Longfellow. 13 sheets (1935); 13 ext. photos (1940, 1963*), 11 int. photos (1963*); 2 data pages (1964*).

Virgin-Coburn House (MASS-871), 7 Dana St. Frame with clapboarding, one-and-a-half stories, gable roof, rear ell, picturesque Gothic-Revival cottage; built 1841, later additions & alterations. 2 ext. photos (1964*), 2 int. photos (1964*); 3 data pages (1964*).

Watson, Daniel, House (MASS-868), 5 Russell Street. Frame with clapboarding, two-and-a-half stories, gambrel roof, ells; built c. 1757. 1 ext. photo (1964*), 2 int. photos (1964*); 3 data pages (1964*).

Whittemore, George, House (MASS-881), 329 Harvard St. Frame with matched siding, two stories, gable roof, ell, octagonal cupola; built 1850. 4 ext. photos (1964*), 3 int. photos (1964*); 3 data pages (1964*).

Wood-Boyd House (MASS-880), 33 Linnaean St. Frame with clapboarding, one-and-a-half stories, mansard roof, rear ell; built 1870. 2 ext. photos (1964*), 1 int. photo (1964*); 3 data pages (1964*).

CARLISLE — *Middlesex County*

Unitarian Church (MASS-537). Frame with clapboarding, two stories with tower and spire; built c. 1811. 1 ext. photo (1941).

CARVER — *Plymouth County. Also No. Carver*

Sturtevant House (MASS-2-96), North Carver Green. Frame with clapboarding and shingles, one story, gambrel roof, rear lean-to; built 1750. 2 sheets (1934); 2 ext. photos (1935).

CHARLESTOWN (See BOSTON)

CHARLTON — *Worcester County*

Towne, General Salem, House (MASS-2-38), see Sturbridge, Mass.

CHATHAM — *Barnstable County*

Atwood, Joseph, House (MASS-161), E. side Atwood St. Wood, one-and-a-half stories; mid 18th C. 7 sheets (1935); 2 ext. photos (1935), 4 int. (1935).

Chatham Windmill (MASS-2-61), E. side of Atwood St. near Mill Pond. Frame with shingles; late 18th C., dilapidated. 5 sheets (1934); 1 ext. photo (1934).

Congregational Church (MASS-428), Old Harbor Rd. & Main St. Frame with clapboarding, wooden spire; early 19th C. 1 ext. photo (1936).

Harding, Enoch, Salt Works (MASS-172), on Buck's Creek near Chatham Bay. Wood; early 19th C. 4 sheets

(1934, 1935); 1 photo of scale model (1935), 2 photocopies of old views (n.d.).

Howes, Captain Solomon, House (MASS-2-62), Queen Anne Road. Frame with shingles, one-and-a-half stories; early 19th C. 4 sheets (1934); 1 ext. photo (1934).

Kimball-Ryder House (MASS-427). Frame with clapboarding, two stories; early 19th C. 1 ext. photo (1935).

Ryder, Christopher, House (MASS-118), N. side State Highway near Ryder's Cove, Chatham Port. Frame with clapboarding, 2 stories; early 19th C. 15 sheets (1934, 1935); 2 ext. photos (1935), 4 int. photos (1935).

Nelson, Colonel John, House (Jennie Sampson House) (MASS-297), Cotchpinnicutt Rd., North Chatham. See Nelson, Colonel John, House (MASS-297); Lakeville, Mass.

Buck House (MASS-2-8), W. of Barn Hill Rd., N. of Buck's Creek, West Chatham. Frame with shingles, one-and-a-half stories; built before 1790. 5 sheets (1934, including barn and outbuildings); 1 ext. photo (1934).

CHELMSFORD — *Middlesex County*

First Congregational Church (MASS-601). Frame with clapboarding and matched siding, recessed Ionic portico, tower and spire; built 1840. 1 ext. photo (1941).

Fiske House (MASS-318), cor. Littleton and Billerica Sts. Frame with clapboarding and pilasters, brick end walls, two stories; built late 18th C. 3 ext. photos (1937), 4 int. photos (1937).

CHELSEA — *Suffolk County*

Captains' Row (MASS-2-37), Marginal and Shurtleff Sts. Series of frame structures with clapboarding, two stories, giant tetrastyle Ionic porticoes; built 1842, later alterations. 2 sheets (1934); 3 ext. photos (1934).

Cary-Bellingham Mansion (MASS-576), 34 Parker St. Museum. Frame with clapboarding, two-and-a-half stories, hipped roof; nucleus built 1659, additions and alterations 1791. 2 ext. photos (1941).

Tucker, Bevis ("Octagon"), House (MASS-579). Frame with clapboarding, two stories, octagonal plan; built mid 19th C. 1 ext. photo (1941).

Way-Ireland-Pratt House (MASS-211), 481 Washington Ave. Frame with clapboarding and shingles, two-and-a-half stories, gambrel roof; built 1660. 14 sheets (1935, 1936).

CHESTER — *Hampden County*

Bascom, Reverend Aaron, House (MASS-112), road to Middlefield. Frame with clapboarding, two stories, side wing; built 1769. 6 sheets (1934); 4 ext. photos (1934, including outbuildings), 3 int. photos (1934).

CLARKSBURG — *Berkshire County*

Musterfield House (MASS-2-25), Middle Rd. Frame with clapboarding, two stories, side wing; built 1805. 6 sheets (1934); 1 ext. photo (1934).

COHASSET — *Norfolk County*

Cushing-Nichols House (MASS-350). Frame with clapboarding and shingles, two stories; built early 19th C., later additions and alterations. 2 ext. photos (1941), 1 photocopy of old photo (n.d.).

First Parish Meetinghouse (MASS-349). Frame with clapboarding, two stories with entry tower and spire, side wing; built early 19th C. 5 ext. photos (1940).

Fitch House (MASS-598). Frame with clapboarding and shingles, one-and-a-half stories; built 18th C., later additions and alterations. 1 ext. photo (1941).

Hobart, Reverend Nehemiah, House (MASS-351). Frame with clapboarding and imitation ashlar siding, two stories, rear wings; built 1722. 6 ext. photos (1936), 4 int. photos (1936).

Shaw-Souther House (MASS-231), Highland Ave. opposite the "Common." Frame with clapboarding, two stories; built 1794, wing added 1854. 16 sheets (1934, 1935).

CONCORD — *Middlesex County*

Brooks, Samuel, House (MASS-819), N. side North Great Rd. (State Rt. 2A), opposite Brooks Rd. Frame with clapboarding, 2 stories, gable and shed roofs; built c. 1747, later additions and alterations. 7 sheets (1961*); 3 ext. photos (1961*), 1 int. photo (1961*); 4 data pages (1961*).

Brown, Reuben, House (MASS-791), 27 Lexington Rd. See Bulkeley, Peter, House (MASS-791); Concord, Mass.

Bulkeley, Peter, House (Reuben Brown House) (MASS-791), 27 Lexington Rd. Frame with clapboarding, two stories, rear wings; built c. 1680. 3 ext. photos (1961*), 2 int. photos (1961*); 2 data pages (1961*).

"Bullet-Hole House" (Jones-Keyes House) (MASS-555), 36 Monument St. Frame with clapboarding, two stories with two-story wing, hipped roof and lean-to; nucleus probably dates from 1664, later additions and alterations. Figured in Battles of Lexington and Concord, 1 ext. photo (c. 1941).

Hunt-Hosmer House (MASS-820), N. side Lowell Rd., about 500′ W. of Liberty St. Frame with clapboarding, two stories; built late 18th C., ell added 1802, later alterations. 2 ext. photos (1961*), 1 int. photo (1961*); 5 data pages (1961*).

Hunt-Hosmer Barn (MASS-821), N. side Lowell Rd., about 550′ W. of Liberty St. Frame with vertical siding, one story, early 18th C. 5 sheets (1961*); 2 ext. photos (1961*), 1 int. photo (1961*); 3 data pages (1961*).

Jones-Keyes House (MASS-555), 36 Monument St. See "Bullet-Hole House" (MASS-555); Concord, Mass.

Meriam House (MASS-822), at Meriam's Corner, about 1 mi. E. of Concord public square. Frame with clapboarding, two stories with two-story rear lean-to; built before 1660. Important during Revolutionary War. 1 ext. photo (1963*).

Old Bank Building (MASS-2-4), N. side Main St., opposite Walden St. Brick, two stories, Doric portico; built 1832. Nathan Hosmer, architect. 5 sheets (1934); 1 ext. photo (1934).

"Old Manse" (Rev. William Emerson House) (MASS-554), W. side Monument Street, about 1/2 mi. N. of Concord public square. Museum. Frame with clapboarding, two-and-a-half stories, gambrel roof, pedimented doorways; built 1769. Later additions and alterations. Nathaniel Hawthorne lived here 1842–46, and named it "Old Manse." 3 ext. photos (1941, 1961*), 4 int. photos (1961*); 6 data pages (1961*).

"Orchard House" (MASS-552), Lexington Rd. Museum. Frame with clapboarding, two-and-a-half stories, central chimney; built 18th C., 19th C. additions and alterations. Home of Louisa May Alcott. 1 ext. photo (c. 1941).

Stowe, Widow, House (MASS-794), N. side of Lexington Rd., .55 mi. E. of cor. of Old Bedford Rd. Frame with shingles, two stories; built c. 1717. 2 ext. photos (1963*).

Taylor, Jacob, House (MASS-792), NW. corner Lexington and Old Bedford Rds. Frame with clapboarding, two stories, rear wing; built early 18th C. 1 ext. photo (1963*).

"The Wayside" (Caleb Ball House) (MASS-551), N. side Lexington Rd., about 1 mi. E. of Concord public square. Museum. Frame with clapboarding, two stories with tower; built early 18th C., 18th and 19th C. additions and alterations. Home of the Alcotts, Hawthornes, and Margaret Sidney. 7 sheets (1961*); 4 ext. photos (c. 1941*, 1961*, 1963*), 3 int. photos (1961*); 11 data pages (1961*).

Wright Tavern (MASS-553), 2 Lexington Rd. Frame with clapboarding, two-and-a-half stories, hipped roof; built 1747, later additions. Important associations with

Revolutionary events of 1774. 6 sheets (1962*); 5 ext. photos (c. 1941*, 1961*, 1963*), 5 int. photos (1963*).

CONWAY — *Franklin County*

Herrick, Joe, House (MASS-2-99), Poland Road. See Parsons, Joel, House (MASS-2-99); Conway, Mass.

Parsons, Joel (Joe Herrick), House (MASS-2-99), Poland Rd. Frame with clapboarding and vertical siding, one-and-a-half stories, rear farm ell; built c. 1775. 7 sheets (1934); 1 ext. photo (1935), 2 int. photos (1935).

DANVERS — *Essex County*

Derby Summerhouse (MASS-783), on Endicott Estate, Ingersoll St., about .4 mi. N. of Center St. Historic house museum. Frame with matched boarding, two stories, Palladian motifs; built 1793–94 for Elias Hasket Derby, Salem merchant; moved from Peabody c. 1901. Samuel McIntire, architect; roof figures carved by John and Simeon Skillin. 5 ext. photos (1960*), 5 int. photos (1960*).

Fowler, Samuel, House (MASS-586), 166 High St. at Liberty. Museum. Brick, 2 stories, hipped roof with deck balustrade; built 1809. 1 ext. photo (1941).

Holton, Judge Samuel, House (MASS-152), 171 Holten St. Frame with clapboarding, 2 stories, rear lean-to and side wing; built 1670, enlarged 1777, 1825. 10 sheets (1935); 4 ext. photos (1936, including 1 photo of privy), 3 int. photos (1936).

Jacobs, George, House (MASS-243), .25 mi. E. of Water St. on Danvers River, about .5 mi. SE. of Danversport.

Frame with clapboarding, 2 stories, rear lean-to; built c. 1658, early additions, demolished c. 1940. 6 sheets (1935, 1936); 10 ext. photos (1937), 7 int. photos (1937), 2 photocopies of photos (c. 1900).

"The Lindens" (King Hooper House) (MASS-2-33), Sylvan St. Frame with clapboarding and rustication, two-and-a-half stories, gambrel roof with balustrade; built 1754, garden laid out c. 1840, moved to Washington, D.C., 1934, rebuilt 1937. Notable interior woodwork. 29 sheets (1934, including garden details); 6 ext. photos (1934), 16 int. photos (1934).

Nurse, Rebecca, House and Garden (MASS-239), 149 Pine St. Frame with clapboarding and shingles, two stories, side wing and rear lean-to; built very late 17th C., house and garden restored c. 1909–12. Rebecca Nurse, wife of the original owner (Francis Nurse), was hanged as a witch in 1692. 2 sheets (1936, 1938, garden details only); 2 ext. photos (1940).

"Oak Knoll" (MASS-205), Summer St. Frame with matched siding, 2 stories, Doric porches; built mid 19th C., garden laid out 1841. John Greenleaf Whittier lived here and named it "Oak Knoll." 3 sheets (1936); 2 ext. photos (1940, including a garden detail).

Porter, Elias Endicott, House and Farm Gates (MASS-289), Locust St. Frame with clapboarding, two stories; built late 18th C. 1 sheet (1938); 3 ext. photos (1940, including details of gates).

Putnam, General Israel, House and Garden (MASS-153), 431 Maple St. at Newburyport Turnpike. Frame with clapboarding, 2 stories, gambrel roof, rear ell; built after 1650, enlarged c. 1744, irregular plan garden laid out c. 1825. Birthplace of General Israel Putnam. 11 sheets (1935, including garden details); 2 ext. photos (n.d.).

Warren, Betsy K., Garden (MASS-290), 124 High St. Informal plan; laid out c. 1870, demolished 1939. 5 sheets (1936, including plot plan and gazebo details).

DARTMOUTH — *Bristol County*

Apponagansett Meetinghouse (MASS-441). Frame with shingles, 2 stories; built late 18th C. 1 ext. photo (1935), 2 int. photos (1935).

DEDHAM — *Norfolk County*

Allin Congregational Church (MASS-568), High St. Frame with clapboarding, two stories with three-stage tower; built 1821. 1 ext. photo (1941).

Fairbanks, Jonathan, House (MASS-223), East St. at Eastern Ave. Historic house museum. Frame with clapboarding, 2 stories; built 1636, later additions. One of the oldest surviving frame houses in the United States. 24 sheets (1939, 1940); 8 ext. photos (1936, 1940*), 20 int. photos (1940*); 1 data page (1930's).

Fisher-Whiting House (MASS-114), 218 Cedar St. Frame with clapboarding, 2 stories; built late 17th or early 18th C., altered mid 18th C. 9 sheets (1934); 3 ext. photos (1937), 4 int. photos (1937).

Haven, Samuel, House (MASS-567), 669 High St. at Ames. Frame with matched siding and brick end walls, two-and-a-half stories with pilasters, one-story Doric

36

porch; built 1795, extensively altered. 2 ext. photos (1941).

Lovell, John M., House (Dedham Inn, Edward M. Richards House) (MASS-258), Court and Highland Streets. Frame with clapboarding, three stories; built 1791, burned 1939. Attributed to Charles Bulfinch, architect. 6 sheets (1939); 1 photocopy of daguerreotype (c. 1857); 4 data pages (1939).

Powder House (MASS-2-66), 162 Ames St. Brick, one story; built 1766, roof restored. 1 sheet (1934); 1 ext. photo (1934).

Richards, Edward M., House (MASS-258). See Lovell, John M., House (MASS-258); Dedham, Mass.

DEERFIELD VILLAGE — *Franklin County*

Barnard-Willard House (MASS-626). See "Old Manse" (MASS-626); Deerfield Village, Mass.

Deerfield Academy (MASS-646). See Memorial Hall (MASS-646); Deerfield Village, Mass.

Dickinson, Captain Thomas, House (MASS-641), W. side Old Deerfield St., near N. end, Lot #8. Frame with clapboarding, two stories, ell; built 1762–64, restored 1907–08. 5 sheets (1959); 4 ext. photos (1959), 1 int. photo (1959); 4 data pages (1959).

Dickinson, David, House (also called the Smith House) (MASS-640), W. side Old Deerfield St., near N. end, Lot #5. Frame with clapboarding, two stories, rear ell; built c. 1790, restored. 8 sheets (1959); 4 ext. photos (1959), 1 int. photo (1959); 3 data pages (1959).

First Church of Deerfield (Brick Church) (MASS-639), W. side Old Deerfield St., at village center. Brick with frame tower, auditorium with gallery; built 1824. Winthrop Clapp, architect. 9 sheets (1959); 3 ext. photos (1935, 1959), 3 int. photos (1959); 1 photocopy of lithograph (c. 1850); 4 data pages (1959).

Frary-Barnard House (MASS-628), Old Deerfield St. Historic house museum. Frame with clapboarding, two stories with lean-to; main section, 1730, addition 1768, interior remodeled c. 1772, restored 1890's. 2 ext. photos (c. 1925); 1 data page (1941).

Lyman, Augustus, House (MASS-625), W. side Old Deerfield St., just S. of Memorial Rd., Lot #14. Frame with clapboarding, 2 stories; built c. 1803. 1 ext. photo (1925, doorway); 2 data pages (1941, 1959).

Memorial Hall (First Deerfield Academy) (MASS-646), N. side Memorial Rd., on part of Lot #27. Museum. Brick, three stories; built 1797–98, 19th C. additions, 1916 wing. Asher Benjamin, architect. 4 sheets (1959); 2 ext. photos (1959), 2 int. photos (1959), 1 photocopy of lithograph (c. 1850); 5 data pages (1959).

Nims, Godfrey, House (MASS-647), NE. corner Old Deerfield St. and Memorial Rd., Lot #28. Frame with brick and clay nogging, clapboarding, 2 stories, ell; built 1718, remodeled 1785. 5 sheets (1959); 3 ext. photos (1959), 2 int. photos (1959); 4 data pages (1959).

"Old Manse" (Barnard-Willard House) (MASS-626), E. side Old Deerfield Street, on Lot #32, opposite brick church. Frame with clapboarding, 2 stories; built 1768. 1 ext. photo (1925, doorway); 1 data page (1959).

Ray, Benjamin, House (MASS-624), W. side Old Deerfield St. between Memorial Rd. and Wells Street, on Lot #14. Frame with clapboarding, two stories, rear ell and lean-to; built 1835. 1 ext. photo (1925); 2 data pages (1941, 1959).

Sheldon, John ("Old Indian"), House (MASS-649); fragments of the original house, demolished in 1848, now in Memorial Hall Museum, Deerfield Village. Originally frame, two stories; built 1698. Considered last survivor of Indian attack 1703–04. 2 sheets (1959*); 2 photos (1959*, doorway), 1 photocopy of daguerreotype (c. 1848*); 18 data pages (1959*, 1960*).

Stebbins, Joseph, House (MASS-652), W. side Old Deerfield St., Lot #10, near village center. Frame with clapboarding, two-and-a-half stories, ell; built c. 1772. 5 ext. photos (1959), 1 int. photo (1959); 3 data pages (1960).

Wells-Thorn House (MASS-653), SE. corner Old Deerfield St. and Memorial Rd., Lot #26. Frame with clapboarding and shingles, two stories, rear ell; nucleus c. 1717, additions 1751, 1783, 1801, restored 1963. 4 ext. photos (1959); 3 data pages (1960).

Williams, Parson John, House (MASS-627), N. side Albany Rd., on part of Lot #13. Frame with clapboarding, two stories, ell, notable Doric frontispiece; built c. 1760, moved to present site 1879. 5 sheets (1959); 4 ext. photos (1925, 1959), 2 int. photos (1959); 4 data pages (1959).

DEERFIELD VILLAGE VICINITY

Allen House–Fuller Studio (MASS-658), W. side of Bars

Rd., 1.9 mi. S. of Deerfield Village. Frame with clap-boarding, two stories, rear ell; built c. 1730, remodeled c. 1880. Artist George Fuller studio. 3 ext. photos (1959), 4 int. photos (1959); 4 data pages (1960).

Locke-Fuller House (MASS-645), E. side of Bars Road, 1.9 mi. S. of Deerfield Village. Load-bearing plank walls with clapboarding, two stories, rear shed ell; built c. 1790. 4 sheets (1959); 2 ext. photos (1959), 2 int. photos (1959); 4 data pages (1959).

Wapping School (MASS-2-81), Greenfield Rd. Frame with clapboarding and matched boarding, one story; built 1839. 1 sheet (1934); 1 ext. photo (1934).

DENNIS — *Barnstable County*

Howes-Jorgenson House (MASS-731), W. side State Rd. 6A, N. of Elm St. Frame with clapboarding, one-and-a-half stories; built between 1766 and 1788. 1 ext. photo (1959*); 3 data pages (1959*).

DIGHTON — *Bristol County*

Baylies, Major Hadijah, House (MASS-431). Frame with clapboarding, 2 stories; built mid 18th C. 1 ext. photo (n.d.).

"Brick" Church (MASS-335). Brick, 1 story with frame tower and spire, Doric tetrastyle portico; built early 19th C. 1 ext. photo (1935).

Coram House (MASS-432). Frame with shingles, two stories, rear ell; built late 18th C. 2 ext. photos (1935).

Delare Cottage (MASS-446). Brick, one story, frame

rear ell, recessed arched doorway; built early 19th C. 2 ext. photos (1935).

Ellery House (MASS-444). Frame with shingles, one story, gambrel roof; built mid 18th C. 1 ext. photo (1935).

"Tulip Tree" House (MASS-445). Frame with clapboarding and shingles, two stories; built early 19th C. 3 ext. photos (1935).

Clouston, Captain John, House (MASS-164), Somerset Ave., North Dighton. Frame with shingles, 1 story, rear ell; built c. 1765. 5 sheets (1935); 1 ext. photo (1935), 2 int. photos (1935).

DORCHESTER (See BOSTON)

DOVER — *Norfolk County*

Caryl Parsonage (MASS-357), Dedham St. near Park Ave. Frame with clapboarding, two stories, rear wings; built late 18th C. 5 ext. photos (1939), 6 int. photos (1937).

Chickering House (MASS-566). Frame with clapboarding, two stories with overhang; built early 18th C. 1 ext. photo (1941).

First Parish Meetinghouse (MASS-565), Springdale Ave. Frame with clapboarding and pilasters, two stories, two-stage tower and small spire; built 1839. 1 ext. photo (1941).

Wentworth, Colonel Paul, House (NH-35). Frame with clapboarding, two stories, rear lean-to; built 1701 in

Salmon Falls, N.H., dismantled, moved, and rebuilt 1936. 41 sheets (1927, 1936); 81 ext. photos (1936), 73 int. photos (1936); 6 data pages (1937).

DUXBURY — *Plymouth County*

"King" Caesar House (MASS-326), King Caesar Rd., Powder Point. Frame with shingles, two stories, hipped roof, side wing; built c. 1798. 5 ext. photos (1938, including one fence detail).

United States Frigate *Constitution*, **Cannon** (MASS-2-84). Cast iron on four-wheeled carriage. 1 photo (1934).

EASTHAM — *Barnstable County*

Doane, Randall, House (MASS-734), S. side Nauset Rd., E. of Salt Pond. Frame with shingles, one-and-a-half stories; built early 19th C. 1 ext. photo (1962*); 3 data pages (1962*).

Doane, Simeon, House (MASS-735), S. of Nauset Rd. near Salt Pond Bay. Frame with shingles, one-and-a-half stories; built late 18th C. 1 ext. photo (1962*); 2 data pages (1962*).

Doane, Sylvanus, House (MASS-712), E. side Nauset Road. Frame with shingles, one-and-a-half stories; built late 18th C. 5 sheets (1960*); 3 ext. photos (1960*), 2 int. photos (1960*); 6 data pages (1960*).

Eastham Windmill (Cape Cod Windmill) (MASS-2-21), Samoset Road, W. of U.S. Rt. 6. Frame with shingles; built late 18th C. 5 sheets (1934); 3 ext. photos (1934, 1935), 4 int. photos (1935).

Higgins House (MASS-433). Frame, one-and-a-half stories; built late 18th C. 1 ext. photo (1936).

Penniman, Captain Edward, House (MASS-693), S. side Fort Hill Rd. near intersection with Governor Prence Rd. Frame with clapboarding, one-and-a-half stories, mansard roof; built 1867–68. 9 sheets (1962*); 4 ext. photos (1962*), 7 int. photos (1962*); 11 data pages (1962*).

Penniman, Captain Edward, Barn (MASS-699), S. side Fort Hill Rd. near intersection with Governor Prence Rd. Frame with clapboarding, one-and-a-half stories, mansard roof; built c. 1870. 4 sheets (1962*); 3 ext. photos (1962*); 3 data pages (1962*).

Prence, Governor Thomas, House (MASS-2-79), E. side King's Highway near corner of "Old Highway." Frame with shingles, one-and-a-half stories; built mid 17th C., destroyed. 1 sheet (1934, conjectural restoration); 1 photocopy of ext. photo (before 1880).

Swift, Nathaniel, House (MASS-736), W. side U.S. Rt. 6, S. of town center. Frame with shingles, one-and-a-half stories; built mid 18th C. 1 ext. photo (1959*); 3 data pages (1960*).

EASTON — *Bristol County*

Old Colony (now New York, New Haven & Hartford) Railroad Station (MASS-663), North Easton. Rough granite, 1 story, hipped roof; commissioned 1881. Henry Hobson Richardson, architect. 3 ext. photos (1959), 1 int. photo (1959); 3 data pages (1960).

EAST NORTHFIELD (See NORTHFIELD VICINITY)

EAST SANDWICH (See SANDWICH)

EAST TAUNTON (See TAUNTON)

EGREMONT — *Berkshire County*

Egremont Academy (MASS-220), E. side Rt. 41 about .11 mi. N. of South Egremont Rd. Frame with clapboarding, two stories with tower; built 1832, since 1882 used as Town Hall. 6 sheets (1935, 1936); 2 ext. photos (1936).

Town Hall (MASS-220), E. side Rt. 41 about .11 mi. N. of South Egremont Rd. See Egremont Academy (MASS-220); South Egremont, Mass.

FAIRHAVEN — *Bristol County*

Bennett, Capt. Thomas, House (MASS-608), 199 Main St. Frame with clapboarding, three stories, hipped roof with balustrade, rear ell; built 1810, altered 1825–30, later additions. 15 sheets (1943–44).

Fish, Reuben, House (MASS-136), NE. corner William and Union Streets. Frame with clapboarding, three stories, hipped roofs with balustrade; built 1831, demolished 1934. 8 sheets (1934, 1935).

Old Academy (MASS-690), Main St. near Huddleston Ave. Frame with shingles, 2 stories with bell tower; built 1798, moved 1906, typical classroom preserved. 2 ext. photos (1961), 2 int. photos (1961); 4 data pages (1961).

FALL RIVER — *Bristol County*

Richard Borden Manufacturing Company No. 1 Mill (MASS-984), East corner Rodman St. and Plymouth Ave. Granite ashlar, 340' (thirty-five bays) x 93'4", five stories, shallow gable roof, two stair towers (northwest and southwest corners); built 1873, Thomas J. Borden, architect. No. 1 Mill considered one of the most efficiently designed mills of its time. 3 sheets (1968, 1971, plans, elevations, section); 6 aerial photos (1968), 5 gen. ext. photos (1968), 4 ext. det. photos (1968), 2 ext. photos of adjacent tenements originally used by mill workers (1968), 1 gen. int. photo (1968), 1 int. det. photo (1968); 7 data pages (1968, 1971).

Durfee Mills (MASS-982), West corner Plymouth Avenue and Pleasant Street. Granite ashlar, twelve buildings (including two principal mills, one secondary mill, office building, boiler houses, picker houses, cotton house and weave sheds), varying from one to five-and-a-half stories, gable and flat roofs, main stair towers No. 1 and No. 2 mills; built 1866 to 1904. 7 sheets (1968, 1971, plans, elevations, sections, details); 5 aerial photos (1968), 15 gen. ext. photos (1968), 4 ext. det. photos (1968), 1 gen. int. photo (1968), 4 int. det. photos (1968); 9 data pages (1968, 1971).

Metacomet Mill (American Print Works No. 6 Mill) (MASS-983), Northeast corner Davol and Anawan Streets. Uncoursed granite, 248'7" (twenty-five bays) x 70'4", six stories, shallow gable roof, main entrance stair tower; built 1847. The oldest existing mill in Fall River. 5 sheets (1968, 1971, plans, elevations, sections, details); 2 aerial photos (1968), 7 gen. ext. photos (1968), 3 ext. detail photos (1968), 1 gen. int. photo (1968), 1 int. detail photo (1968); 7 data pages (1968, 1971).

Union Mills (MASS-981), Southeast corner intersection of Pleasant Street and I-195, Interchange #12. Granite (except for one brick building), nine buildings (including two mills, picker houses, engine houses, boiler house, waste house and office building), varying from one to six stories, gable, shallow gable and flat roofs; built 1859 to 1895, Josiah Brown, principal architect. 7 sheets (1968, 1971, plans, elevations, sections, details), 4 aerial photos (1968).

FALL RIVER VICINITY — *Bristol County*

Barnaby, James, House (MASS-2-27), E. side South Main St., about .5 mi. N. of Fall River–Freetown town line, Freetown. Frame with clapboarding and shingles, two stories; built before 1740, burned 1935. 8 sheets (1934); 2 ext. photos (1934), 3 int. photos (1934).

FITCHBURG — *Worcester County*

Cushing Flour and Grain Mill (MASS-896), near Laurel Street bridge. Random ranged ashlar masonry, three-and-a-half stories with cupola; built c. 1868. 2 ext. photos (1930's*).

FRAMINGHAM — *Middlesex County*

Boston and Albany Railroad Station (MASS-666). Random ashlar masonry, one story; commissioned 1883. Henry Hobson Richardson, architect. 3 ext. photos (1959), 2 int. photos (1959); 3 data pages (1960).

Eames, Jonathan, House ("Old Red House") (MASS-324), Union Ave. Frame with clapboarding, two stories, hipped roof, side and rear wings; built mid 18th C. 3 ext. photos (1940).

46

First Baptist Church (MASS-320). Frame with clapboarding, two stories with four-stage tower & spire; built early 19th C. 3 ext. photos (1940, including carriage shed).

Framingham Academy (MASS-2-16), cor. Vernon & Grove Sts., Framingham Center. Random coursed granite ashlar, two stories, tetrastyle masonry column portico; built 1837. 3 sheets (1934); 1 ext. photo (1934).

Gates House (MASS-286), Gates St. Frame with clapboarding, two stories; built 1774. 1 ext. photo (1940).

Kellogg House (MASS-359), Kellogg St. Frame with clapboarding, two stories, gambrel roof; built mid 18th C. 3 ext. photos (1938), 2 int. photos (1938).

Nixon, Colonel Thomas, House (MASS-247), 881 Edmands Road. Frame with clapboarding, 2 stories, rear lean-to; built 1785–88, 1 photocopy of old photo (n. d.).

Pike-Haven-Foster House (MASS-616), corner of Grove and Belknap Sts. Frame with clapboarding, two stories, gambrel roof; nucleus dates from late 17th C., early additions. 7 sheets (1956); 3 ext. photos (1938).

FRAMINGHAM VICINITY

Howe-Gregory House (MASS-238), Wayside Inn Rd. Frame with clapboarding, one-and-a-half stories, gambrel roof; built mid 18th C. 3 ext. photos (1938).

FRANKLIN — *Norfolk County*

Little Red Schoolhouse (MASS-450). Brick, one story; built mid 19th C. 2 ext. photos (1941).

GEORGETOWN — *Essex County*

House (MASS-449), 36 East Main St. Frame with clapboarding, two-and-a-half stories, one-story Doric entry porch; built early 19th C. 2 ext. photos (1930's).

Nelson, Captain Bill, House Fence (MASS-254), 8 Elm St. (South Green). Turned wooden posts and pickets; built 1840. 1 sheet (1937–38); 2 photos (1937).

White Horse Tavern Fence (MASS-253), 108 E. Main St. Turned wooden posts and pickets; built 1840. 1 sheet (1937–38); 1 photo (1938).

GILL — *Franklin County*

Red House (MASS-2-60), French King Highway, Riverside. Frame with clapboarding, one-and-a-half stories, rear ell; built c. 1745. 5 sheets (1934); 1 ext. photo (1934), 3 int. photos (1934).

GLOUCESTER — *Essex County*

First Universalist Church (Independent Christian Church) (MASS-451), Middle St. Frame with clapboarding, two stories with four-stage tower; built 1774. 7 ext. photos (1939), 9 int. photos (1939).

School House (MASS-453). Frame with clapboarding, one story; built early 19th C. 2 ext. photos (1939).

Custom House (MASS-2-12), River Rd., Annisquam. Frame with shingles, one-and-a-half stories, gambrel roof; built c. 1720. 2 sheets (1934); 2 ext. photos (1934).

Hodgkin, William, Tide Mill (MASS-2-92), Washington

St., Annisquam. Frame with clapboarding, two stories, side wing; built 1833. 3 sheets (1934); 7 ext. photos (1940), 2 int. photos (1940).

Lobster Cove (MASS-115), Annisquam. Frame buildings and wharves of early fishing harbor; built 1720–1820. 6 sheets (1934, including perspective and plan).

GRANVILLE — *Hampden County*

Curtis Tavern (MASS-221), State Rt. 57. Frame with clapboarding, two stories; built 1765, later additions and alterations. 2 ext. photos (1930's*), 2 int. photos (1930's, 1930's*), 1 photocopy of old ext. photo (n.d.).

GREAT BARRINGTON — *Berkshire County*

Dwight, General Joseph (William Cullen Bryant), House (MASS-360), near junction of U.S. Rt. 7 and State Rt. 23. Frame with clapboarding, two stories, rear lean-to; built 1739. 5 ext. photos (1937), 5 int. photos (1937).

GREENBUSH (See SCITUATE)

GREENFIELD — *Franklin County*

Coleman-Hollister House (MASS-2-19), Bank Row. Frame with clapboarding and giant Ionic pilasters, two stories, hipped roof; built 1796. Asher Benjamin, architect. 20 sheets (1934); 5 ext. photos (1934), 5 int. photos (1934).

Gould-Potter House (MASS-642), 486 Main St. at High. Brick, two stories with giant Ionic portico and side wings; built 1827, 20th C. alterations. Elija T. Hayden, probably designer. 3 sheets (1959); 7 ext. photos (1940*, 1959), 3 int. photos (1959); 4 data pages (1959).

Leavitt-Hovey House (now Greenfield Public Library) (MASS-656), 402 Main St. Frame with clapboarding, two stories, side pavilions; built 1797. Asher Benjamin, architect. 4 ext. photos (1959); 3 data pages (1960).

Newton, Reverend Roger, House (MASS-2-94), Newton Place. Frame with clapboarding, two-and-a-half stories, hipped roof; built 1793, moved from corner of Newton Place and Court St. 1848. 8 sheets (1934); 2 ext. photos (1934).

GREENFIELD VICINITY

McHard House (MASS-2-45), 2.5 mi. from Greenfield on U.S. Route 5. Frame with clapboarding, 1 story, rear lean-to; built before 1730, destroyed. 1 sheet (1934); 1 ext. photo (1934).

GROTON — *Middlesex County*

Prescott, Dr. Oliver, Milestones (MASS-203), Farmers Row & Main St., Great and Old Ayer Rd. 5 slate milestones and 1 granite boulder; erected 1787 by Dr. Prescott. 7 sheets (1936); 6 photos (1940).

Robbins, Andrew, House (MASS-603). Frame with clapboarding, two stories, partial gambrel roof, rear lean-to; built mid 18th C., alterations. 2 ext. photos (1941).

HADLEY — *Hampshire County*

Huntington House (Porter-Phelps-Huntington House) (MASS-361), on State Rt. 47. Frame with clapboarding, two-and-a-half stories, gambrel roof, extensive L-shaped rear wing; built mid 18th C. 5 ext. photos (1935), 5 int. photos (1935).

Keefe, John, Tobacco Barns (MASS-113), Old Hadley St. Frame with vertical siding, one story; built c. 1890, destroyed 1936. 1 sheet (1934); 1 ext. photo (1935).

Porter-Phelps-Huntington House (MASS-361), on State Rt. 47. See Huntington House (MASS-361), Hadley, Mass.

Porter, Samuel, House (MASS-2-53), West St. Frame with clapboarding, 2 stories with overhang; built 1713. 11 sheets (1934); 3 ext. photos (1934), 2 int. photos (1934).

Porter Store (MASS-158), Old Hadley St. Frame with matched siding and clapboarding, pilasters, 2 stories; built c. 1840, altered. 3 sheets (1935); 1 ext. photo (1935).

Woodbridge, Colonel Ruggles, House (MASS-180), 26 Woodbridge Street. Frame with clapboarding and quoins, two-and-a-half stories, gambrel roof; built 1788. 18 sheets (1935); 1 ext. photo (1935), 7 int. photos (1935).

Wright House (MASS-182), 96 College St. Frame with clapboarding, two stories; built c. 1820. 8 sheets (1935); 2 ext. photos (1935), 1 int. photo (1935).

HALIFAX — *Plymouth County*

Fence (MASS-328). Square wooden posts with four wooden horizontal rails between each. 1 photo (1938).

Standish, Shadrach, House (MASS-2-70), Monponsett St. Frame with shingles, one-and-a-half stories; built 1730. 3 sheets (1934); 2 ext. photos (1934), 2 int. photos (1934).

Wood, Timothy, House (MASS-362). Frame with shingles, one-and-a-half stories, rear ell; built mid 18th C., later alterations. 4 ext. photos (1935, 1936), 7 int. photos (1935).

HAMILTON-IPSWICH — *Essex County*

Warner's Bridge (MASS-251), Mill Rd. over Ipswich River. Irregular three-arched ashlar; built 1856, 1937 additions and alterations. Henry Hubbard, architect. 1 sheet (1938); 4 photos (1937).

HANCOCK — *Berkshire County*

Hancock Shakers (MASS-721), U.S. Rt. 20, W. of intersection with State Rt. 41. A Shaker community organized late 18th C., active until mid 20th C. 2 ext. photos (c. 1931*, 1962*).

Hancock Shakers' Brethren's Shop (MASS-722), S. of U.S. Rt. 20, about .24 mi. W. of intersection with State Rt. 41. Frame with clapboarding, two stories; built before 1833. 6 ext. photos (1939*, 1962*), 4 int. photos (1962*); 2 data pages (1962*).

Hancock Shakers' Dairy and Weave Shop (MASS-692), S. of U.S. Rt. 20, about .24 mi. W. of intersection with State Rt. 41. Frame with clapboarding, two-and-a-half stories; built first half 19th C. 9 sheets (1960*).

Hancock Shakers' Main Dwelling (MASS-723), S. of

52

U.S. Rt. 20, about 1/4 mi. W. of intersection with State Rt. 41. Brick, three-and-a-half stories; built 1830. 6 ext. photos (1939*, 1962*), 24 int. photos (1931*, 1939*, 1962*).

Hancock Shakers' Meetinghouse (originally Shirley Shakers' Meetinghouse) (MASS-724), N. of U.S. Rt. 20, about 1/4 mi. W. of intersection with State Rt. 41. Frame with clapboarding, one-and-a-half stories, hipped roof; built 1792–93 at Shirley, Mass., Shaker community, moved to Hancock community 1962. Built by Moses Johnson. 5 ext. photos (1962*), 2 int. photos (1962*); 2 data pages (1962*).

Hancock Shakers' Ministry's Shop (MASS-725), N. of U.S. Rt. 20, about 1/4 mi. W. of intersection with State Rt. 41. Frame with clapboarding, two stories; built by 1820. 2 ext. photos (1939*).

Hancock Shakers' Round Barn (MASS-674), S. of U.S. Rt. 20, about .2 mi. W. of intersection with State Rt. 41. Rubble masonry and frame with clapboarding, 3 stories with monitor; built 1826. 2 sheets (1945*); 11 ext. photos (1939*, 1962*), 5 int. photos (1931*, 1962*); 2 data pages (1962*).

Hancock Shakers' Shop, Laundry, & Waterworks Building (MASS-730), S. of U.S. Rt. 20, about .3 mi. W. of intersection with State Route 41. Frame with clapboarding, three-and-a-half stories; built 1790. 9 sheets (1963*); 8 ext. photos (1939*, 1962*), 12 int. photos (1930's*, 1939*, 1962*); 2 data pages (1962*).

Hancock Shakers' Sisters' Shop (MASS-726), S. of U.S. Rt. 20, about .23 mi. W. of intersection with State Rt. 41. Frame with clapboarding, two-and-a-half stories;

built early 1800's. 6 ext. photos (1962*), 2 int. photos (1962*); 2 data pages (1962*).

Hancock Shakers' Tan Shop (MASS-727), S. of U.S. Rt. 20, about .2 mi. W. of intersection with State Rt. 41. Rubble masonry and frame with clapboarding, two-and-a-half stories; built 1835. 7 ext. photos (1939*, 1962*), 2 int. photos (1962*); 1 data page (1962*).

Hancock Shakers' Trustees' Building (MASS-728), S. of U.S. Rt. 20, about .15 mi. W. of intersection with State Rt. 41. Frame with clapboarding, 2 stories; built 19th C. 1 ext. photo (1939*).

Hancock Shakers' Wash House, Building #4 (MASS-729), S. of U.S. Rt. 20, about .24 mi. W. of intersection with State Rt. 41. Brick, one story; built 19th C. 3 ext. photos (1962*), 1 int. photo (1962*).

HANOVER CENTER — *Plymouth County*

Stetson, Samuel, House (MASS-611), Hanover St. Frame with shingles, two stories, rear ell; built c. 1694, later additions and alterations. 6 sheets (1943–44).

HARVARD — *Worcester County*

Harvard Shakers Church Family (MASS-862), about 1.0 to 1.2 mi. S. of State Rt. 2A along Shaker Rd. The Church Family, one of several families of Harvard Shakers, grew out of Mother Ann Lee's proselytizing efforts in Massachusetts in the late 18th C. 1 photocopy of George Kimball's 1836 plot plan.

Harvard Shakers Church Family Barn Ruins (MASS-861), 1.0 mi. S. of State Rt. 2A, about .06 mi. off W. side of Shaker Rd. Remnants of stone foundations and stone walls; built probably c. 1830, burned 1935. Before destruction, building was wood frame with stone foundations and stone walls at first level (five levels in all). 2 sheets (1964*), 4 ext. photos (1963*).

Harvard Shakers Church Family Meetinghouse (MASS-806), E. side Shaker Road, about 1.1 mi. S. of State Rt. 2A. Frame with clapboarding, two-and-a-half stories, side and rear wings; built 1791. 5 ext. photos (1963*), 2 int. photos (1963*).

Harvard Shakers Church Family Ministry (Ministry's Shop) (MASS-807), E. side Shaker Rd., about 1.1 mi. S. of State Rt. 2A. Frame with brick veneer, 2 stories; built 1847. 4 sheets (1963*); 3 ext. photos (1963*), 5 int. photos (1963*).

Harvard Shakers Church Family Office Building (MASS-809), E. side Shaker Rd., 1.2 mi. S. of State Rt. 2A. Frame with clapboarding, three-and-a-half stories, rear wing; built probably c. 1835. 6 ext. photos (1963*), 4 int. photos (1963*).

Harvard Shakers Church Family Second House (MASS-810), W. side Shaker Rd., 1.2 mi. S. of State Rt. 2A. Frame with clapboarding, two stories; built 1795. 5 ext. photos (1963*), 1 int. photo (1963*).

Harvard Shakers Church Family Square House (Shadrach Ireland House) (MASS-804), E. side of Shaker Rd., about 1.0 mi. S. of State Rt. 2A. Frame with clapboarding, two-and-a-half stories, rear wing; built 1769. Shadrach Ireland, builder. 5 ext. photos (1963*), 2 int. photos (1963*).

55

Harvard Shakers Church Family Tailor Shop (MASS-805), East side Shaker Rd., about 1.0 mi. S. of State Rt. 2A. Frame with clapboarding, one story, rear wing; built probably c. 1830. 2 ext. photos (1963*).

Harvard Shakers South Family Barn (MASS-808), N. side of S. Shaker Rd., about .8 mi. E. of State Rt. 110. Rubble masonry, three stories; built 1835. 4 sheets (1963*); 8 ext. photos (1940*, 1963*), 8 int. photos (1940*, 1963*).

Harvard Shakers South Family Dwelling (MASS-888), about .7 mi. E. of State Rt. 110 on N. side of S. Shaker Road. Frame with clapboarding, three stories with cupola; built c. 1835. 6 ext. photos (1940*, 1963*), 2 int. photos (1963*).

Harvard Shakers South Family Laundry (MASS-889), about .7 mi. E. of State Rt. 110 on N. side of S. Shaker Rd. Frame with clapboarding, two-and-a-half stories, connected by rear ell to South Family Dwelling. 1 ext. photo (1963*).

Harvard Shakers South Family Shop Building #1 (MASS-890), about .7 mi. E. of State Rt. 110 on N. side of S. Shaker Rd. Frame with stucco (now asphalt) shingles, two-and-a-half stories; built probably c. 1800. 1 ext. photo (1963*), 3 int. photos (1963*).

Harvard Shakers South Family Shop Building #2 (MASS-891), about .7 mi. E. of State Rt. 110 on N. side of S. Shaker Rd. Frame with brick veneer, two stories; built probably c. 1830, partially destroyed. 4 ext. photos (1963*).

Ireland, Shadrach, House (MASS-804). See Harvard

Shakers Church Family Square House (MASS-804); Harvard, Mass.

HATFIELD — *Hampshire County*

Billings, Cornelia, House (MASS-454). Frame with clapboarding, 2 stories; built early 19th C. 2 ext. photos (1935).

Billings, Lieutenant David, House (MASS-166), 77 Main St. Frame with clapboarding, 2 stories, hipped roof; built 1783. 11 sheets (1935); 1 ext. photo (1938), 2 int. photos (1938).

Morton House (MASS-2-73). See Partridge, Cotton, House (MASS-2-73); Hatfield, Mass.

Partridge, Cotton (Morton), House (MASS-2-73), corner Bridge Lane and Lower Main St. Frame with clapboarding, 2 stories, rear lean-to and ell; built before 1725. 6 sheets (1934); 2 ext. photos (1934).

HAVERHILL — *Essex County*

Dustin, Thomas, House (MASS-273), Hillsdale Ave. Brick, two stories; built 1696–97, partially restored. 4 ext. photos (1938).

HINGHAM — *Plymouth County*

Beal, John, House (MASS-364). Frame with clapboarding, 2 stories, rear wing; nucleus built 1690, early additions. 2 ext. photos (1936), 2 int. photos (1936).

Cushing House (MASS-2-85), South Pleasant St. Frame with shingles, two stories, rear ell and additions; built

1720. 12 sheets (1934); 5 ext. photos (1934), 4 int. photos (1934).

First Parish Meetinghouse (MASS-595). See Old Ship Church (MASS-595); Hingham, Mass.

Lincoln, General Benjamin, House (MASS-363). Frame with clapboarding, two stories, rear wing; built mid 18th C. 2 ext. photos (1936), 11 int. photos (1936).

Lincoln, Perez, House (Old Garrison House) (MASS-600), 123 North St. Frame with clapboarding, two stories, rear wing; nucleus built mid 17th C., early additions. Moved to Cape after 1941. 1 ext. photo (1941), 4 int. photos (1941).

Lincoln, Samuel, Cottage (MASS-620), 182 North Street. Frame with clapboarding, one-and-a-half stories with two-story ell; built 18th C., early additions. Built by ancestor of Abraham Lincoln. 2 sheets (1945).

Loring, Thomas, House (MASS-366). Frame with clapboarding, two stories, twin entry frontispieces, rear wings; built mid 18th C. 3 ext. photos (1941).

New North Meetinghouse (MASS-422), near North and Lincoln Sts. Frame with clapboarding and pilasters, two stories, square tower with cupola; built c. 1806. Attributed Charles Bulfinch, architect. 3 ext. photos (1941).

Old Ship Church (First Parish Meetinghouse) (MASS-595), 88 Main St. Frame with clapboarding, unique open roof trusses, galleries; small deck with bell turret; built 1681, enlarged and remodeled 1731, 1755, 1792, restored 1930. Only surviving 17th C. New England church. 11 sheets (1960); 17 ext. photos (1941, 1961*), 20 int. photos

(1959*, 1961*), 3 photocopies of an early lithograph and 2 int. views (n.d.).

Pilgrim Cottage (MASS-455). Frame with clapboarding, one-and-a-half stories, gambrel roof; built late 18th C. 1 ext. photo (1936).

Shute, Daniel, House (MASS-197), corner Main and S. Pleasant Sts. Frame with shingles and imitation ashlar, 2 stories, hipped and gambrel roofs; built 18th C., later rear ell addition. 21 sheets (1935, 1936); 7 ext. photos (1935), 8 int. photos (1935).

Wilder, Jabez, House (MASS-137), Main St., South Hingham. Frame with clapboarding, one-and-a-half stories, side and rear wings; built 1690. 10 sheets (1934, 1935); 4 ext. photos (1936), 6 int. photos (1936).

IPSWICH — *Essex County*

Appleton, William (Sally Choate), House (MASS-607). Frame with clapboarding, two-and-a-half stories with overhang, gambrel roof; built 1766, later alterations, demolished 1944. 5 sheets (1943–44).

Caldwell, Waldo, House (MASS-462), High St. Interior details only; built c. 1692. Notable early woodwork. 6 int. photos (1938).

Choate Bridge (MASS-2-69), Rt. 1A over Ipswich River. Fieldstone and ashlar, two arched; built 1764. 1 sheet (1934); 2 photos (1934, 1940).

Congregational Parsonage Fence (MASS-255), 19 North Main Street. Remains of wooden fence set on granite wall, square posts with Ionic pilasters; built c. 1790. 1 sheet (1937–38).

Dane, Doctor Philemon, House and Fence (MASS-256), 41 S. Main St. Frame with clapboarding, two-and-a-half stories, gambrel roof; built c. 1716, fence undated. 2 sheets (1937, 1938); 3 ext. photos (1940, including fence details).

Heard, John, House (MASS-321), on State Rt. 1A. Frame with clapboarding, three stories, hipped roof, rear wings; built 1795. 3 ext. photos (1940, including fence detail).

House (MASS-461), 40 N. Main St. Frame with clapboarding, 3 stories, hipped roof; built early 19th C. 2 ext. photos (1936, 1940, showing adjacent two-story frame structure with wide overhang).

Howard-Emerson House (MASS-423), Turkey Shore Rd. Museum. Frame with clapboarding, two stories with overhang; built late 17th C., early additions. 2 ext. photos (n.d.), 1 int. photo (n.d.).

Kimball, John, House (MASS-177), 75 High St. Frame with clapboarding, two stories, rear lean-to; built c. 1700. 5 sheets (1936); 3 ext. photos (1935), 7 int. photos (1935).

Norton-Corbett (Matthew Perkins) House (MASS-457), 8 East Street. Frame with clapboarding, two stories with overhang, rear lean-to; built 1701–09, early additions. 3 ext. photos (1936).

Old Post Office (MASS-456). Frame with clapboarding,

two stories with overhang; built late 18th C. 2 ext. photos (1937).

Perkins, Matthew, House (MASS-457), 8 East Street. See Norton-Corbett House (MASS-457); Ipswich, Mass.

Proctor House (MASS-322), Jeffrey's Neck Rd. Frame with clapboarding, two-and-a-half stories; original portion built 1680's, later additions and alterations, dismantled 1939 and oldest section re-erected at present site. 11 ext. photos (1940), 1 int. photo (1940).

Treadwell House (MASS-368). Frame with clapboarding, 2 stories, hipped roof; built late 18th C. 1 ext. photo (1940).

Wade, Colonel Nathaniel, House (MASS-458). Frame with clapboarding, two-and-a-half stories, gambrel roof, two-and-a-half story rear wing; built 1727. 2 ext. photos (1940).

Whipple, John, House (MASS-460), 53 S. Main St. Museum. Frame with clapboarding, 2 stories with overhang; built 1640, early additions. 1 photo (1940).

JAMAICA PLAIN (See BOSTON)

KINGSTON — *Plymouth County*

Bradford, Major John, House (MASS-2-78), corner Maple St. and Landing Rd. Frame with shingles, two stories, rear lean-to and wing; built late 17th C. 6 sheets (1934); 3 ext. photos (1935), 4 int. photos (1935).

Holmes House (MASS-369). Frame with clapboarding, 2

stories, hipped roof, rear wing; built late 18th C. 3 ext. photos (1935).

Sever, Squire William, House and Garden (MASS-135), 2 Linden St. Frame with clapboarding, hipped roof with balustrade, extensive side and rear wings; built 1760. 25 sheets (1934, 1935, 5 sheets garden detail); 6 ext. photos (1936), 13 int. photos (1936).

Willett, Captain Thomas, House (MASS-370). Frame with shingles, two stories, rear lean-to and wing; built mid 18th C. 7 ext. photos (1937, including outbuildings), 2 int. photos (1937).

LAKEVILLE — *Plymouth County*

Nelson, Colonel John, House (Jennie Sampson House) (MASS-297), Main St. Frame with shingles and clapboarding, two stories, rear wing; built c. 1770, moved after 1936 (to Cotchpinnicut Rd., North Chatham, Mass.), altered. 6 ext. photos (1936), 3 int. photos (1936).

Sampson, Jennie, House (MASS-297), Main St. See Nelson, Colonel John, House (MASS-297); Lakeville, Mass.

Ward, George, House (MASS-2-20), Crooked La. Frame with shingles, one-and-a-half stories, gambrel roof, extensive rear and side wings; built 1712. James Sproat, architect. 6 sheets (1934); 1 ext. photo (1934), 1 int. photo (1934).

LANCASTER — *Worcester County*

First Parish Church (MASS-542), facing the Common. Brick, 2 stories with two-stage tower and cupola, giant arcuated portico; built 1816. Charles Bulfinch, architect. 4 ext. photos (1941, including carriage shed).

LANESBOROUGH — *Berkshire County*

First Baptish Church (MASS-463). Brick, 1 story with tower and open bell housing; built late 18th C. 1 ext. photo (1935).

Registry of Deeds Building (MASS-372). Irregular ashlar, one story; built early 19th C. 2 ext. photos (1937).

LEE — *Berkshire County*

Merrell Tavern (MASS-622), Main St., South Lee. Brick, frame third story with clapboarding, double tiered Tuscan porch, rear wing; built 1760, early 19th C. additions. 5 sheets (1945).

LEXINGTON — *Middlesex County*

Buckman Tavern (MASS-547), Bedford St. Museum. Frame with clapboarding, two-and-a-half stories, hipped roof; nucleus late 17th C., later additions & alterations. Associated with Battle of Lexington. 9 sheets (1962*); 3 ext. photos (1941, 1963*).

Follen Unitarian Church (Octagon Church) (MASS-590). Frame with clapboarding, one story, octagonal plan with belfry and spire; built 1840. 1 ext. photo (1930).

Hancock-Clarke House (MASS-549), 35 Hancock St. Museum. Frame with clapboarding, two stories; ell built 1698, main block 1734, restored and relocated (from across street) 1896. Important in Battle of Lexington. 7 sheets (1962*); 4 ext. photos (1941, 1963*).

Harrington, Jonathan Jr., House (MASS-548), corner Elm and Bedford Sts. Frame with clapboarding, two stories, hipped roof; built mid 18th C. 1 ext. photo (1941).

Munroe Tavern (MASS-550), 1332 Massachusetts Ave. Museum. Frame with clapboarding, 2 stories, rear ell; nucleus dates from 1695, 18th C. additions. Washington entertained here 1789. 7 sheets (1962*); 3 ext. photos (1941, 1963*).

Robbins-Stone House (MASS-609), 669 Massachusetts Ave. Frame with clapboarding, 2 stories, rear lean-to; built 1740, later additions and alterations, moved c. 1946–47 to 1268 Massachusetts Ave. 5 sheets (1943–44).

Stone Building (Cary Memorial Library) (MASS-605), 1874 Massachusetts Ave. Frame with clapboarding, two stories, giant Doric portico; built mid 19th C. 2 ext. photos (1941).

Whittemore, Jacob, House (MASS-823), 21 Marrett St. Frame with clapboarding, 2 stories; built prior to 1756, later additions and alterations. 9 sheets (1961*); 3 ext. photos (1961*), 2 int. photos (1961*); 1 photocopy of photo (c. 1915*); 6 data pages (1961*).

LINCOLN — *Middlesex County*

Barn (MASS-793), E. side Old Concord Rd., .4 mi. from Concord Rd. Frame with shingles and clapboarding, one story and loft, rear wing; built early 19th C. 1 ext. photo (1963*), 2 int. photos (1963*).

Brooks, Daniel, House (MASS-824), E. side Brooks Rd., about .75 mi. N. of Cambridge Turnpike (Rt. 2). Frame with clapboarding and shingles, two stories, rear ell; built c. 1695, later additions and alterations. 3 sheets (1962*); 2 ext. photos (1963*).

Brooks, Joshua, House (MASS-825), S. side North Great Rd., about .15 mi. W. of Old Bedford Rd. Frame with clapboarding, 2 stories, rear ell; built c. 1730. 11 sheets (1961*); 2 ext. photos (1961*), 4 int. photos (1961*); 2 data pages (1961*).

Brooks Tavern (Hartwell-Rogers House) (MASS-826), S. side Great North Rd., E. of Brooks Rd. Frame with clapboarding, brick end walls, 2 stories; built prior to 1791, later rear additions. 8 sheets (1961*), 4 ext. photos (1961*), 3 int. photos (1961*); 6 data pages (1961*).

Brown, Nathan, House (MASS-827), E. side Tower Rd., about .63 mi. S. of Baker Bridge Rd. Frame with clapboarding, two stories; built c. 1720, later additions and alterations. 4 sheets (1962*); 2 ext. photos (1963*).

Hartwell, Samuel, House (MASS-828), N. side Virginia Rd., about .19 mi. NW. of intersection with North Great Rd. Frame with clapboarding, two stories; built probably in early 18th C., later additions. 2 ext. photos (1961*), 3 int. photos (1961*).

Hartwell Tavern (MASS-829), N. side Virginia Rd., W. of Bedford Lane. Frame with clapboarding, 2 stories; built 1692, appendage 1732. Important during British retreat from Concord, 1775. 11 sheets (1961*); 5 ext. photos (1961*), 4 int. photos (1961*); 5 data pages (1961*).

Nelson, John, House (MASS-830), N. of Great North Rd., about 1.25 mi. E. of intersection with Nelson Rd. Frame with clapboarding, two stories, side wings; kitchen built in 18th C., main section 1811, later additions. John Nelson, builder. 6 sheets (1962*).

Nelson, John, Barn (MASS-831), N. of Great North Rd., about 1.25 mi. E. of intersection with Nelson Rd. Frame with shingles, one story. 1 ext. photo (1963*), 2 int. photos (1963*).

Nelson, Josiah, House (MASS-832), N. side Nelson Rd., about .15 mi. E. of Lexington Town Line. Frame with clapboarding, brick end walls, rear and side walls; built early 19th C. Built by John Nelson, carpenter, for his father, Josiah, a famous Lincoln Minuteman. 4 ext. photos (1961*), 2 int. photos (1961*); 5 data pages (1961*).

Smith, Captain William, House (MASS-833), East of Virginia Road, near intersection with North Great Rd. Frame with clapboarding, two stories, rear ell; built late 17th C., later additions and extensive alterations. Home of Revolutionary War hero. 1 ext. photo (1963*).

LONGMEADOW — *Hampden County*

Colton, Captain Gideon, House (MASS-2-36), 1028 Longmeadow Street. Frame with clapboarding, two stories, rear wings; built 1796. Attributed to Asher Benjamin, architect. 13 sheets (1934); 4 ext. photos (1934), 4 int. photos (1934).

Field, Colonel Alexander, House (MASS-173), 280 Longmeadow St. Frame with clapboarding, two stories,

66

hipped roof, rear ell; built 1794. 14 sheets (1934); 6 ext. photos (1937), 3 int. photos (1937).

LOWELL — *Middlesex County*

Bowers, Jarathmael, House & Barns (MASS-525). Frame with clapboarding, one story; built early 19th C. 2 ext. photos (1941), 1 int. photo of barn (1941).

Chelmsford Glass Works' Tenement House (MASS-327). Frame with clapboarding and shingles, 1 story; built late 18th C. 1 ext. photo (1938).

Middlesex Canal (Lowell Canal) (MASS-380), remains of canal that ran from Somerville to Lowell. First American canal of the type familiar in England and on the Continent. Structures of regular ashlar; Lock-Keeper's House at Wilmington now shingled, two stories; opened 1803. 14 ext. photos (1938); 1 photocopy of old view of Medford Bridge (n.d.).

Whistler, James Abbott McNeill, Birthplace (MASS-526), 243 Worthen St. Museum. Frame with clapboarding, two-and-a-half stories, rear ell; built 1824. 1 ext. photo (1941).

LUDLOW-WILBRAHAM — *Hampden County*

Covered Bridge (MASS-497), over Chicopee River. Wood with 2 masonry abutments and one pier; built mid 19th C. 2 ext. photos (1937).

MANCHESTER — *Essex County*

Forster, Major Israel, House (MASS-373), on State Rt. 127. Frame with clapboarding, 2 stories with monitor;

67

built late 18th C. 12 ext. photos (1938, 1939, including outbuilding & farm implements), 3 int. photos (1938, 1939).

Lee, Ma'm, House (MASS-323), 39 Forest St. Frame with clapboarding, one-and-a-half stories, gambrel roof; built c. 1725, repaired and altered 1940. 7 sheets (1940–41); 5 ext. photos (1940), 1 int. photo (1940).

Orthodox Congregational Church (MASS-268), cor. Central & Church Sts. Frame with clapboarding, one story with balcony, three-stage bell tower; built 1809. 10 ext. photos (1938, 1939), 2 int. photos (1938).

MARBLEHEAD — *Essex County*

Hooper, Robert ("King"), House (MASS-249), 8 Hooper St. Frame with clapboarding, shingles, and wooden imitation ashlar, 3 stories, three-and-a-half story rear ell with gambrel roof; built 1745, ell earlier. Notable interior woodwork. 27 sheets (1936); 5 ext. photos (1936), 27 int. photos (1936).

Jayne, Peter, House (MASS-374), 37 Mugford St. Frame with clapboarding, two stories; built early 18th C. 1 ext. photo (1936), 9 int. photos (1935).

Lee, Colonel Jeremiah, Mansion (MASS-859), 161 Washington Street. Frame with rusticated facade, three stories, hipped roof with cupola, Ionic porch; built 1768. Elaborate interiors with notable paneling. 1 ext. photo (1930's*), 2 int. photos (1930's*).

Old Gun (Artillery) House (MASS-186), 45 Elm St. Brick, one story, pyramidal roof; built c. 1800. 3 sheets (1935, 1936); 2 ext. photos (1937).

Powder House (MASS-2-67), Green St. Brick, 1 story, circular "ogee" roof; built 1775. 1 sheet (1934); 1 ext. photo (1934).

Town House (MASS-2-6), Market Sq. Frame with clapboarding, two stories on high basement; built 1727. 6 sheets (1934); 2 ext. photos (1934).

Trevett, Captain Samuel, House (MASS-104), 65 Washington St. Frame with clapboarding, 2 stories, rear lean-to; built c. 1750. 14 sheets (1934); 1 ext. photo (1934), 8 int. photos (1934).

Waters, William, House and Bakery (MASS-2-31), Washington Street, Market Sq. Frame with clapboarding, 2 stories, gambrel roof, rear bakeshop ell and side wing; built 1683, demolished 1937. 12 sheets (1934); 5 ext. photos (1934, 1937), 5 int. photos (1934).

MARION — *Plymouth County*

First Universalist Church (MASS-241), cor. Pleasant and Main Sts. Frame with clapboarding, two stories, square tower; built 1832. 7 sheets (1935, 1936).

MARSHFIELD — *Plymouth County*

Hatch, Walter, House (MASS-375). Frame with shingles, two stories, side wings; built mid 18th C. 3 ext. photos (1936), 2 int. photos (1936).

Thomas, Anthony, House (MASS-376). Frame with clapboarding and shingles, two stories, rear ell; built late 18th C. 3 ext. photos (1936), 1 int. photo (1936).

Weatherbee, George H., House (MASS-377). Frame

with shingles, two stories, hipped roof, side wing; built early 19th C. 5 ext. photos (1936, including fence details), 5 int. photos (1936).

Winslow House (MASS-815). Frame with clapboarding, 2 stories, rear wings; built late 17th C. 2 ext. photos (1936), 3 int. photos (1936).

Clift, Nathaniel, House (MASS-207), Spring St., Marshfield Hills. Frame with shingles, two stories, hipped roof, side wing; built 1705, later alterations. 19 sheets (1935); 1 ext. photo (1936).

MEDFIELD — *Norfolk County*

Clark, Seth ("Peak"), House (MASS-2-77), State Rt. 109. Frame with shingles, one-and-a-half stories; built 1680, restored. 2 sheets (1934); 2 ext. photos (1934).

MEDFORD — *Middlesex County*

Blanchard, George, House (MASS-2-5), 14 Bradbury Ave. Frame with clapboarding and shingles, two stories, gambrel roof, rear lean-to; built 1657–58. 5 sheets (1934); 2 ext. photos (1934), 2 int. photos (1934); 1 photocopy of photo (c. 1900).

Brooks, Captain Caleb, House (MASS-229), 24 Woburn St. Frame with clapboarding, two stories; built before 1765. 6 sheets (1935); 2 int. photos (1940).

Brooks, Jonathan, House (MASS-144), cor. Woburn and High Sts. Frame with shingles (originally clapboarding), two stories, gambrel roof, rear ell; built 1796, later alterations. 9 sheets (1934); 4 ext. photos (1936), 2 int. photos (1936), 1 photocopy of photo (c. 1890).

Hall, Andrew, House (MASS-159), 45 High St. Frame with clapboarding, three stories; built c. 1727, demolished 1939. 1 sheet (1935); 1 ext. photo (1934, showing row of three Hall Houses on High St.).

Hall, Benjamin Jr., House (MASS-2-56), 57 High St. Frame with clapboarding, two-and-a-half stories, hipped roof; built 1785, demolished 1938. 24 sheets (1934); 2 ext. photos (1934), 2 int. photos (1934).

Hall, Ebenezer, House (MASS-261), 49 High St. Frame with clapboarding, brick end walls, three stories; built 1785, demolished 1939. 10 sheets (1934).

Lawrence House (MASS-246), 353 Lawrence Rd. Frame with clapboards, two-and-a-half stories, three separate structures joined; built before 1785, later additions and alterations. 14 sheets (1935).

Magoun, Thatcher, House (MASS-194), 117 High St. Frame with vertical siding and clapboarding, two stories, Ionic porticoes, rear wing; built 1835, later additions, demolished before 1965. 11 sheets (1936); 3 ext. photos (1935), 2 photocopies of int. photos (c. 1900).

Osgood, Reverend David, House (MASS-111), 141 High St. Frame with clapboarding, 2 stories; built 1785. 17 sheets (1934); 2 ext. photos (1934), 2 int. photos (1934).

Royall, Isaac, House (MASS-577). See Usher-Royall House; Medford, Mass.

Sawyer, Nathan, Cottage (MASS-219), 306 Riverside Ave. Frame with clapboarding and shingles, one-and-a-half stories, rear ell; built before 1830. 6 sheets (1936); 3 ext. photos (1937).

Usher-Royall House (MASS-577), W. side Main St., between George and Royall Sts. Brick and frame with clapboarding and wooden imitation masonry, three stories, giant pilasters and classic window and door pediments; originally late 17th C. brick house, remodeled and enlarged 1733–37, 1747–50. 12 ext. photos (1940, 1941, 1961*), 1 photocopy of old photo (n.d.).

Usher-Royall Forecourt Fence (MASS-130A), West side Main St., between George & Royall Streets. Wooden capped posts and pickets, low brick wall; built mid 18th C., demolished. 1 sheet (1940); 1 photocopy of early view (n.d.).

Usher-Royall Garden House (MASS-129), W. of (behind) Usher-Royall House, West of Main St., between George & Royall Streets. Frame, octagonal, one story; built c. 1739–75, demolished. 4 sheets (1934), 1 ext. photo (1935, remaining wall), 2 photocopies of old photos (c. 1890, n.d.).

Usher-Royall Slave Quarters (MASS-130), 15 George Street. Brick and frame with clapboarding, two stories; built c. 1732–39. 11 sheets (1934); 3 ext. photos (1935), 3 int. photos (1935).

MELROSE — *Middlesex County*

Lynde, Ensign Thomas, House (MASS-464). Frame with clapboarding, two-and-a-half stories, gambrel roof, rear wing; built mid 18th C., demolished by 1965. 3 ext. photos (1940).

Upham, Phineas, House (MASS-489), 253 Upham St. Museum. Frame with clapboarding, 2 stories, rear lean-to; built 1703, later additions. 10 sheets (1943–44); 2 ext. photos (1941).

MENDON — *Worcester County*

First Parish Unitarian Church (MASS-242), corner Maple and Elm Sts. Frame with clapboarding, two stories with four-stage tower and spire, giant tetrastyle Tuscan portico; built 1820, fire damage 1937. Elias Carter, architect. 20 sheets (1936); 7 ext. photos (1937, 1940, including carriage shed).

MIDDLEBOROUGH — *Plymouth County*

Central Methodist Church (MASS-2-68), Cherry St. Frame with shingles, 1 story; built 1831. 2 sheets (1934); 1 ext. photo (1934).

Eddy, Zachariah, Law Office (MASS-851). See West Springfield, Mass.

First Congregational Church Carriage Sheds (MASS-2-39), Plympton St. Frame with vertical siding, one story; built 1828, ruinous. 1 sheet (1934); 8 ext. photos (1936).

Mill House (MASS-379), 30 Jackson St. Frame with shingles, one-and-a-half stories, rear lean-to, single unit; built early 19th C. 3 ext. photos (1936).

Mill Houses (MASS-379), 20–22 Jackson St. Frame with clapboarding, one-and-a-half stories, rear lean-to, double unit; built early 19th C. 1 ext. photo (1936).

Mill Houses (MASS-379), 24, 26, 28 Jackson St. Frame

73

with clapboarding and shingling, one and one-and-a-half stories, attached single and double units; built early 19th C. 4 ext. photos (1936).

Mill Houses (MASS-379), 32–34 Jackson St. Frame with shingles, one-and-a-half stories, rear lean-to, double unit; built early 19th C. 1 ext. photo (1936).

Mill Houses (MASS-379), 36–38 Jackson St. Frame with shingles, one-and-a-half stories, double unit; built early 19th C. 1 ext. photo (1936).

Old Tavern Inn (MASS-2-40), (Rt. 28) Wareham St. Frame with shingles, one and two stories; built c. 1690, additions c. 1763. 4 sheets (1934); 2 ext. photos (1934, 1937), 6 int. photos (1934, 1937).

Peirce, Colonel P. H., Store (MASS-2-7), N. Main St. Frame with clapboarding and shingles, two stories with one-story side wings, giant tetrastyle Doric portico; built 1808, altered for use as courthouse 1936. 9 sheets (1934); 3 ext. photos (1934), 6 int. photos (1934), 1 photocopy of old ext. photo (n.d.).

Peirce, L. T., Store (MASS-2-28), corner N. Main and Jackson Sts. Frame with clapboarding, one story, three-column Tuscan porch; built c. 1800. 2 sheets (1934); 1 ext. photo (1934).

Robinson, E., Store (MASS-2-29), corner N. Main and Jackson Sts. Brick, two stories; built c. 1840. 1 sheet (1934); 1 ext. photo (1934).

Sampson, Deborah, House (MASS-2-49), 280 Wareham Street. Frame with clapboarding and shingles, one story, rear lean-to; built late 18th C., ruinous. 1 sheet (1934); 1 ext. photo (1937).

Sproat House (MASS-378). Frame with clapboarding, 2 stories, side wing; built early 19th C. 4 ext. photos (1936, including stable), 5 int. photos (1936).

Thompson, Venus, House (MASS-2-64), Thompson St. Frame with clapboarding and shingles, one story, rear wings; built c. 1700. 3 sheets (1934); 1 ext. photo (1934).

Wood, Judge, Office (MASS-198), 123 S. Main St. Frame with clapboarding, one story, one room; built c. 1785. 2 sheets (1936); 1 ext. photo (1935), 1 int. photo (1935).

Wood, Silas, House (MASS-331). Frame with clapboarding, one-and-a-half stories, gambrel roof, side and rear wings; built early 18th C. 2 ext. photos (1936), 1 photocopy of old ext. photo (n.d.).

MIDDLETON — *Essex County*

Bradstreet House (MASS-587). Frame with clapboarding, one story, gambrel roof, side wing; built early 18th C. 2 ext. photos (1941).

MILLVILLE — *Worcester County*

Covered Bridge (MASS-440). Frame with vertical siding; built early 19th C., dilapidated. 4 photos (1941).

MILLVILLE VICINITY

Chestnut Hill Meetinghouse (MASS-122), Chestnut Street. Frame with clapboarding, 2 stories; built 1769. 20 sheets (1935); 5 ext. photos (1935), 7 int. photos (1935).

MILTON — *Norfolk County*

Belcher, Governor Jonathan, House and Garden (MASS-196), 401 Adams St. Frame with clapboarding, two stories, hipped roof, built 1776; semiformal garden, laid out 1781. 9 sheets (1936); 4 ext. photos (1940).

Davenport, Isaac, House (MASS-465). Frame with clapboarding, two stories with deck balustrade; built early 19th C., additions. 1 ext. photo (1940).

Holbrook, Dr. Amos, House Garden (MASS-232), 203 Adams St. Formal garden with central path and series of terraces; laid out 1801. 4 sheets (1937).

Howe, Joseph N., House (MASS-138), 597 Randolph Ave. Wedge-shaped ashlar, one-and-a-half stories; built c. 1830. 6 sheets (1935); 2 ext. photos (1936).

Hutchinson, Governor Thomas, House and Garden (MASS-168), 195 Adams St. Frame with clapboarding, two-and-a-half stories; house and garden date from mid 18th C., demolished mid 20th C. 6 sheets (1935); 3 ext. photos (1940).

Powder House (MASS-2-66), 781 Canton Ave. Brick, one story; built 1812. 1 sheet (1934); 1 ext. photo (1934).

Shepard-Hinckley House (MASS-613), 264 Brook Rd. Frame with clapboarding, two stories, rear ell, side shed and front wing; built 1805, later additions, demolished 1944, shed relocated in Ipswich. 7 sheets (1943–44).

Vose, Daniel, House ("Suffolk Resolves House") (MASS-2-13), 1370 Canton Ave. Frame with clapboarding, two stories, hipped roof, Doric porch; built 1774, moved from 38 Adams St. c. 1955. 6 sheets (1934); 2 ext. photos (1934), 1 int. photo (1934).

MONTAGUE — *Franklin County*

Covered Bridge (MASS-101), over Connecticut River, Montague City. Wood on two masonry abutments and four piers, 770 feet long; built 1870, destroyed 1936. 4 sheets (1934); 2 ext. photos (1934), 1 int. photo (1934).

NANTUCKET — *Nantucket County*

Barrett, John Wendell House (also known as "Wallace Hall") (MASS-915), 72 Main Street. Wood frame with clapboards, five-bay front, two-and-a-half stories with cupola and ell, hipped roof, central hall, Greek revival details; built 1820, John Coleman, builder. 4 ext. photos (1965); 3 int. photos (1965); 4 data pages (1965).

Bunker, Reuben R., House (MASS-916), Academy Hill. Wood frame with clapboards and shingles, five-bay front, two stories, central door, central chimney, Federal portico and trim; built c. 1806, portico added c. 1820. 3 ext. photos (1968); 3 data pages (1966).

Cary, Edward, House (MASS-855), 117 Main St. Frame with shingles, two stories, hipped roof; built c. 1800. 1 ext. photo (1962*), 2 int. photos (1962*); 2 data pages (1965*).

Coffin, Henry, House (MASS-811), 75 Main St. Brick, two-and-a-half stories with cupola, rear two-story wing; built 1833. 2 ext. photos (1962*), 2 int. photos (1962*); 2 data pages (1965*).

Coffin, Jared, House (also known as the Ocean House)

(MASS-918), 29 Broad St. Brick, five-bay front, three stories with cupola, central hall plan, end chimneys, roof parapet, built 1845, Ocean House Hotel 1847–1961, restored by Nantucket Historical Trust 1961, open year round as a hotel. 6 ext. photos (1969); 4 data pages (1965).

Coffin, Jethro, House (also known as "Oldest House") (MASS-919), Sunset Hill, off West Chester St. (Lat. 41° 17′ 16″ N., Long. 70° 6′ 15″ W.). Frame with wood shake exterior, 39′2″ (three-bay front) x 30′7″, one-and-a-half stories with garret, gable roof with lean-to, central door, central chimney, leaded casement windows; built 1686, restored 1927 by William Sumner Appleton and Alfred F. Shurrocks. Oldest house on Nantucket. National Register of Historic Places. 10 ext. photos (1965, 1969), 9 int. photos (1965, 1969), 3 photocopies of photographs (1 c. 1880, 2 prior to 1927), 6 data pages (1969).

Coffin, Joshua, House (MASS-1004), 52 Centre St. Frame with shingles, 37′7″ x 30′9″, five bays, two-and-one-half stories, gable roof, lean-to, central door, central chimney; built ca. 1750s. 11 sheets (1969) including plans, elevations, details (isometric of plank frame window, isometric of framing and chimney core); 4 ext. photos (1966, 1969), 8 int. photos (1966, 1969), 10 data pages (1969).

Coffin, Major Josiah, House (MASS-911), 60 Cliff Rd. Wood frame with shingles, 38′5½″ (five-bay front) x 30′10″ plus appendage, two stories, gable roof, rear lean-to, central door, central chimney; built 1724. 9 sheets (1967, including plans, elevations, sections, details); 3 ext. photos (1966), 7 int. photos (1966); 7 data pages (1965, 1971).

Coffin-Athearn Stores (MASS-906), 2 Union St. Brick 41′4¾″ (six-bay east and west elevations) x 34′3″, two stories, gable roof, irregular plan for stores and offices; built prior to 1836, altered after fire 1846, made into one building 1884. 3 sheets (1966, plan, elevations); 2 ext. photos (1966); 6 data pages (1966, 1971).

Coffin-Gardner House (MASS-854), 33 Milk St. Frame with shingles, two-and-a-half stories, gable roof, rear wings; built 1820. 2 ext. photos (1962*), 3 int. photos (1962*); 2 data pages (1965*).

Coleman, Elihu, House (MASS-2-86), Hawthorne Lane. Frame with shingles, two stories, rear lean-to and ell; built 1722. 10 sheets (1934); 1 ext. photo (1935), 4 int. photos (1935).

Fence and Porch Details (MASS-614), various premises. Wood; early 19th C. 1 sheet (1944–45).

First Congregational Church (MASS-902), 62 Centre Street. Frame, 62′8″ x 90′3″ plus tower projection 8′1″, auditorium plan, one story with tower; built 1834, steeple removed c. 1840, remodeled 1852 with Gothic Revival details and trompe l'oeil painting, complete restoration and replacement of steeple 1968–69. 8 sheets (1966, incl. locational map, plans, elevations, sections, details); 3 ext. photos (1966, before restoration), 2 ext. photos (1968, after restoration), 1 ext. photo (1970, after restoration), 3 int. photos (1966, before restoration), 6 int. photos (1970, after restoration), 3 photocopies of c. 1900 photos, 1 photocopy of c. 1934 drawing; 6 data pages (1966).

Fish Houses (MASS-853), N. and S. sides Old South Wharf. Frame with shingles, one and two stories, gable roofs; built 19th C., many moved from other locations. 2 ext. photos (1962*), 2 int. photos (1962*); 2 data pages (1965*).

Gardner, George, House (MASS-858), 8 Pine St. Frame with shingles, 1 story, gambrel roof; built c. 1750. 1 ext. photo (1962*), 1 int. photo (1962*); 3 data pages (1965*).

Gardner, Richard, House (MASS-839), 32 West Chester St. Frame with shingles, two-and-a-half stories, gable roof, rear lean-to and ell; built c. 1724. 2 ext. photos (1962*), 5 int. photos (1962*); 3 data pages (1965*).

Hadwen-Wright House (MASS-905), 94 Main St. Wooden frame with clapboards, 30'1" (three-bay front) x 40'3½", ell 10'5" x 14'1½", two stories with full basement, garret and cupola, tetrastyle Corinthian portico, gable roof, Greek Revival details, plaster domes in ballroom and stairhall second floor, spring floor in ball room; built 1845, Frederick Brown Coleman, carpenter. 10 sheets (1966, incl. plans, elevations, sections, details); 6 ext. photos (1966), 1 ext. photo (1968), 8 int. photos (1966); 9 data pages (1966).

House (MASS-195), 19 Hussey Street. Frame with shingles, two stories, rear lean-to; side wing. 2 ext. photos (1937).

House (unidentified) (MASS-856). Details of leaded-glass window now in Fair Street Museum; built mid 18th C. 1 sheet (1962*).

India Street Neighborhood Study (MASS-1013), 15–45 (north side only) India Street (between Centre and Liberty Streets). Sixteen separate frame houses with shingle or clapboard siding. Built between 1785 and

1830, they form a continuous street facade providing an example of typical Nantucket residential streetscape and architecture as it existed at the turn of the century. 12 sheets (1970, plans, elevations, sections, details, streetscapes); 12 exterior photos (1970); 8 data pages (1970).

Mitchell, William, Meridian Stones (MASS-183), Main and Fair Streets. Two marble stones to indicate true meridian line; erected 1840. 2 sheets (1936).

Nantucket Athenaeum (MASS-812), N. side Lower Pearl St. at Federal. Frame with matched siding and pilasters, two stories, gable roof, recessed Ionic portico; built 1847. Frederick Coleman, believed to be architect. 2 ext. photos (1962*), 3 int. photos (1962*); 3 data pages (1965*).

Old Gaol (MASS-120), Vestal St. (Jail Lane). Log covered with shingles, two stories; built 1711, moved and rebuilt 1805. 5 sheets (1935); 1 ext. photo (1935).

Orange and Union Sts. Neighborhood Study, Pierce, Easton, Russell, Bunker, Gardner Houses (Orange St. Block) (MASS-947), 15, 17, 19, 21 and 23 Orange St. Row houses, wood frame with clapboards, 120′ x 83′, gable roof, two-and-a-half stories, ell, side hall plan; built 1831. 8 sheets (1970, Easton House, plans, elevations, sections); 12 ext. photos (1965, 1968, 1970), 6 int. photos (1965, 1970); 7 data pages (1965, 1970); see Orange and Union Sts. Neighborhood Study (MASS-1014) (1970, plan, elevation, streetscape).

Orange and Union Streets Neighborhood Study, Starbuck, Levi, House (James Codd House) (MASS-912), 14 Orange St. Wood frame with flush horizontal siding in panels between pilasters, 41' (six-bay front) by 62', 2 stories, gable roof, ell, modified central hall plan; built c. 1837. 10 sheets (1967, plans, sections, elevations); 2 ext. photos (1968, 1970); 7 data pages (1965, 1970); see Orange and Union Streets Neighborhood Study (MASS-1014) (1970, plan, elevation, streetscape).

Pacific Club (MASS-836). See Rotch, William, Building (MASS-836); Nantucket, Mass.

Raymond-Coleman House (MASS-837), 53 Orange St. Frame with shingles, two-and-a-half stories, gable roof, rear lean-to and wing; probably built c. 1802, restored. 1 ext. photo (1962*), 2 int. photos (1962*); 2 data pages (1965*).

Rotch, William, Building (now Pacific Club) (MASS-836), Main St. at head of Straight Wharf. Brick, 3 stories, gable roof with captains' walk; built 1772, bought by Pacific Club 1861. 1 ext. photo (1962*), 3 int. photos (1962*); 5 data pages (1965*).

Sanford, Frederick C., House Garden (MASS-162), Federal, Broad, and Water Sts. Formal garden; laid out 1847. 5 sheets (1935).

Second Congregational Meeting House (Unitarian-Universalist) (MASS-838), W. side Orange St. opposite Stone Alley. Frame with shingles, two stories, gable roof, three-story front with three-stage tower and cupola; built 1809, Elisha Ramsdell, master builder; new tower replaced original in 1830; extensive alterations, 1844, F. B. Coleman, architect; restored 1957–64. Notable interior decorative painting by Carl Wendte. 2 ext. photos (1962*), 4 int. photos (1962*); 4 data pages (1965*).

Starbuck, Joseph, Houses (known as the "Three Bricks") (MASS-941), 93, 95 and 97 Main St. 3 separate houses, each one, brick, five-bay front, two stories, hipped roof, cupola and parapet, two chimneys each end, central hall plan; built 1838, James Childs, builder, Christopher Capen, master-mason. 6 ext. photos (1966); 5 data pages (1965).

Starbuck, Thomas, Homestead (MASS-942), 11 Milk St. Wood frame with shingles, four-bay front, two stories with two story ell, gable roof with lean-to, off-center door, off-center chimney; built c. 1761, moved to present site c. 1790, ell 1913, restored 1931. 3 ext. photos (1966); 3 data pages (1966).

Swift, Henry, House Garden (MASS-167), 91 Main St. Formal garden; laid out 1823. 2 sheets (1935).

Windmill ("East Mill") (MASS-141), North Mill and South Mill Sts. Museum. Frame with shingles, octagonal plan; built 1746. 5 sheets (1934); 3 ext. photos (1935).

"Auld Lang Syne" (Captain Henry Coleman House) (MASS-857), Siasconset Bank, Siasconset. Frame with shingles, one story; built late 17th C., later additions and extensive alterations. Probably the oldest structure on Nantucket. 2 sheets (1962*).

Cary, Betsy, Cottage (Captain William Baxter House or "Shanunga") (MASS-610), Mitchell Street, Siasconset. Frame with shingles, one-and-a-half stories; built 1682, moved from Sesachacha Pond, addition 1782. 2 sheets (1943–45).

83

NATICK — *Middlesex County*

Wilson, Henry, Shoe Shop (MASS-176), corner West Central and Mill Sts. Frame with clapboarding, one story, one room plan; built c. 1825. Shop of Henry Wilson, Vice President of United States. 1 sheet (1936); 2 ext. photos (1937, 1938), 2 int. photos (1938).

NEW BEDFORD — *Bristol County*

Congregational (now First Unitarian) Church (MASS-681), NW. corner Union and Eighth Sts. Granite ashlar, one story, three-aisled Gothic hall plan; built 1836–38. A. J. Davis and Russell Warren, architects. 4 ext. photos (1961), 2 int. photos (1961), 3 photocopies of 2 old photos (n.d.) and 1 early ext. lithograph (n.d.); 6 data pages (1961).

Custom House (MASS-682), SW. corner Second and Williams Sts. Granite ashlar, two stories, hipped roof; built 1834–37. Robert Mills, architect; also attributed to Russell Warren. 3 ext. photos (1961), 3 int. photos (1961); 7 data pages (1961).

Friends Meetinghouse (MASS-467), North side Spring Street near Sixth. Brick, two stories; built 1824. 2 ext. photos (1935), 1 int. photo (1961); 2 data pages (1961).

Grinnell, Joseph, Mansion (now St. John's Roman Catholic Convent and Academy) (MASS-675), 379 County St. Granite ashlar, three stories, giant Doric portico; built 1836, altered for convent and academy use. Attributed to Russell Warren, architect. 2 ext. photos (1961), 2 int. photos (1961); 5 data pages (1961).

Harrison, John, Building (MASS-686), 23 Centre St.

Granite rubble with brick facade, four stories; built c. 1820, interior altered for warehouse. 1 ext. photo (1961); 2 data pages (1961).

Institution for Savings (MASS-684), Second and Williams Sts. Ashlar and brick, one story, Greek Revival detailing; built 1853, now a machine shop. Russell Warren, architect. 2 ext. photos (1961); 4 data pages (1961).

Merchants' and Mechanics' Banks Building (MASS-683), 56–62 N. Water St. Brick, two stories, giant Ionic portico, originally two separate banks; built 1831–35, first floor altered 19th C. Russell Warren, architect. 2 ext. photos (1961), 2 int. photos (1961); 5 data pages (1961).

Rodman, Samuel Jr., House (MASS-466), SE. corner Spring and County Sts. Brick and stucco, three stories with cupola; built 1827. 1 ext. photo (1935); 1 data page (1961).

Rodman, William R., House (MASS-676), 388 County St. Granite ashlar, three stories, giant Corinthian portico; built 1833, altered mid 19th C. and c. 1900. 2 ext. photos (1961), 2 int. photos (1961); 6 data pages (1961).

Rotch, William J., House (MASS-678), 19 Irving St. Frame with matched siding, two-and-a-half stories, Gothic Revival; built 1846, moved 1928 from 103 Orchard St. A. J. Davis and William R. Emerson, architects. 3 ext. photos (1961), 4 int. photos (1961), 2 photocopies of early watercolors (n.d.); 17 data pages (1961).

Rotch, William Jr., House (Mariners' Home) (MASS-

679), 15 Johnny Cake Hill. Frame and brick, three stories, hipped roof; built c. 1790, moved 1850. 2 ext. photos (1961), 2 int. photos (1961); 4 data pages (1961).

Russell, Charles, Building (MASS-687), NW. corner Union and Water Sts. Brick and stone, three stories; built 1828, interior altered into warehouse. 1 ext. photo (1961); 2 data pages (1961).

Seaman's Bethel (MASS-680), W. side Johnny Cake Hill. Frame with shingles, 2 stories; built 1832, rebuilt 1867 with tower. Linked romantically with whaling and *Moby Dick*. 1 ext. photo (1961); 2 data pages (1961).

Taber, Henry, House (MASS-677), 115 Orchard St. Frame with clapboarding, two stories, Corinthian order entrance and porch; built 1846. 3 ext. photos (1961), 2 int. photos (1961); 3 data pages (1961).

Tallman, William, Warehouse (MASS-685), 106 N. Front St. Brick and hewn timber framing, three-and-a-half stories; built c. 1790, lower floors altered. 1 ext. photo (1961), 2 int. photos (1961); 3 data pages (1961).

Wamsutta Mill (MASS-987), Acushnet Ave. Brick, buildings vary in height from one to four stories; gable, saw-tooth and flat roofs; stair and service towers on east side of main building along Acushnet Ave; built 1847 onward; first textile mill in New Bedford; first large textile mill designed for steam power. 8 ext. photos (1968).

Warehouse (MASS-688), SW. corner N. Front St. and Rose Alley. Granite ashlar, 3 stories; built first half 19th C. 2 ext. photos (1961); 4 data pages (1961).

Warehouse (MASS-689), SE. corner Union and Front Sts. Granite ashlar and brick, four-and-a-half stories; built mid 19th C. 1 ext. photo (1961); 2 data pages (1961).

NEWBURY — *Essex County*

Coffin, Tristram, House (MASS-472), 14 High Rd. Museum. Frame with clapboarding, two stories, rear wings; built c. 1651, early additions. 1 ext. photo (1940).

Jackman, Richard, House (MASS-471), N. of lower Green. Frame with clapboarding, one story; built 1696, moved from river site and restored. 1 ext. photo (1940).

Short House (Nathaniel Knight House) (MASS-468), 33 High Rd. Frame with clapboarding, 2 stories, rear wing; built 1717, additions 1732–40. 2 ext. photos (1940).

Swett-Ilsley House (MASS-300), 4–6 High Rd. Frame with clapboarding, two stories; built 1670, additions and alterations, 1700, 1760. 1 ext. photo (1940), 1 int. photo (1934).

Toppan, Dr. Peter, House (MASS-469). Frame with shingles, 2 stories with overhang, gambrel roof; built 1697, later additions and alterations. 1 ext. photo (1940).

NEWBURYPORT — *Essex County*

Cushing, John N., House and Garden (MASS-213), 98 High Street. Brick, three stories with monitor; formal garden; built 1808, garden laid out by John Cushing 1830. 7 sheets (1936); 6 ext. photos (1940).

Gaol, Gaoler's House, and Barn (MASS-121), corner

Auburn and Vernon Sts. Regular granite ashlar, two and two-and-a-half stories (house); built 1825. 12 sheets (1934); 5 ext. photos (1934), 3 int. photos (1934).

Globe Steam Mills (MASS-295), Federal St., between Liberty and Water Sts. Brick, three stories with stair tower; built 1845, demolished 1940. 15 sheets (1940); 4 ext. photos (1940).

Hennesey House (MASS-2-82), 2 Summer St. Frame with clapboarding, two stories, gambrel roof; built 1760, later additions, burned 1934. 4 sheets (1934); 2 ext. photos (1934).

Highway Cut-off Demolition (MASS-117), between Winter and Summer Sts., High and Merrimac Sts. Structures built between 1725 and 1815. 6 sheets (1934, plans and elevations before demolition); 10 ext. photos (1934).

Marden House (MASS-2-87), 32 Summer St. Frame with clapboarding and shingles, 2 stories, rear wings; built 1765–70, demolished 1934. 6 sheets (1934); 3 ext. photos (1934), 3 int. photos (1934).

Meetinghouse of First Religious Society (MASS-473, 623), Pleasant St. Frame with clapboarding, two stories with four-stage tower & spire; built 1801. Attributed to Timothy Palmer, architect. 1 sheet (1945); 4 ext. photos (1940).

Moulton, Joseph, House and Garden (MASS-216), 89–91 High St. Frame with clapboarding, three stories, double house; "double hourglass" formal garden; house built 1809, garden laid out 1840. 6 sheets (1936); 5 ext. photos (1940, including gazebos).

Pierce, Benjamin, House and Garden (MASS-236), 47 High St. Frame with clapboarding, three stories with balustrade; narrow, central-path garden with three terraces; built 1811–12, laid out c. 1815. 9 sheets (1936, 1937, garden details only); 3 ext. photos (1940).

Regan House (MASS-110), 7 Birch St. Frame with clapboarding, three stories, hipped roof; built c. 1815, demolished 1934. 3 sheets (1934); 2 ext. photos (1934).

Semple House (MASS-2-93), 176 High St. Frame with clapboarding, three stories, hipped roof; built early 19th C., demolished 1934. 6 sheets (1934).

Stocker, Ebenezer, House Garden (William Wheelwright Garden) (MASS-209), 75 High St. Circular formal garden with less formal axial garden to rear; laid out 1841. Henry V. Ward, designer. 6 sheets (1936).

Stockman, Charles, House (MASS-140), 31–33 Winter St. Frame with clapboarding and shingles, 2 stories, rear lean-to and wing; built 1770–80, demolished 1934. 5 sheets (1934); 4 ext. photos (1934), 2 int. photos (1934).

Stockman House (MASS-2-95), 5 Birch St. Frame with clapboarding, two stories, rear ell; built 1740, demolished 1934. 2 sheets (1934); 3 ext. photos (1934).

Stonecutting Shop (MASS-2-97), rear of 2 Summer St. Frame with shingles and clapboarding, one-and-a-half stories; built early 19th C., demolished 1934. 1 sheet (1934); 2 ext. photos (1934).

Thibault House (MASS-123), 8 Summer St. Frame with clapboarding, three stories, hipped roof; built c. 1815, demolished 1934. 5 sheets (1934); 1 ext. photo (1934).

Thurlow House (MASS-2-83), 43 Winter St. Frame with clapboarding, two stories, rear lean-to; built c. 1725, demolished 1934. 3 sheets (1934); 2 ext. photos (1934), 1 int. photo (1934).

Wheelwright, Abraham, House and Garden (MASS-780), 77 High Street. Brick, three stories with balustrade and octagonal cupola; built c. 1810, garden laid out 1841. 8 ext. photos (1940, including gazebos).

NEW MARLBOROUGH — *Berkshire County*

Harmon, Lieutenant, House (MASS-386). Frame with clapboarding, 2 stories; built early 19th C. 1 ext. photo (1935).

NEW SALEM — *Franklin County*

Allen, Samuel C., House (MASS-846), E. side S. Main St., about .1 mi. S. of E. Main St. Frame with clapboarding, 2 stories; built between 1809 and 1816. 2 ext. photos (1940*), 3 int. photos (1940*).

NEWTON — *Middlesex County*

Boston and Albany Railroad Station (MASS-665), Auburndale. Ashlar masonry, one story; commissioned 1881, demolished by 1965. Henry Hobson Richardson, architect. 2 ext. photos (1959), 3 int. photos (1959); 3 data pages (1960, 1961).

Boston and Albany Railroad Station (MASS-667), 1897 Washington St., Woodland. Random ashlar, 1 story, hipped roof; commissioned 1884, demolished by 1965. Henry Hobson Richardson, architect. 2 ext. photos (1959), 1 int. photo (1959); 3 data pages (1960).

Crehore Paper Mill (MASS-545), 375 Elliot Street. Fieldstone, 1 story with basement; built early 19th C., additions. 1 ext. photo (1941).

Jackson, Timothy, House and Garden (MASS-139), 527 Washington Street. Frame with clapboarding, brick end walls, two stories, hipped roof; built 1809. 13 sheets (1934); 8 ext. photos (1935, including 2 fence details), 4 int. photos (1935).

Kendrick House (MASS-387), 302 Waverly Ave. Frame with clapboarding, 2 stories, gambrel roof, rear lean-to; built late 18th C. 2 ext. photos (1935), 8 int. photos (1935, 1939).

Mill House No. 1 (MASS-545), Chestnut St. Frame with clapboarding, two stories; built early 19th C. 4 ext. photos (1938).

Mill House No. 2 (MASS-388), Chestnut St. Frame with clapboarding, two stories, one-story side wing; built early 19th C. 2 ext. photos (1938).

Mill House No. 3 (MASS-388), Sullivan Ave. Frame with clapboarding, two stories, gable and hipped roof; built early 19th C. 3 ext. photos (1938).

Mill House No. 4 (MASS-388), Chestnut St. Frame with clapboarding, one-and-a-half stories, rear ell, double dwelling; built early 19th C. 2 ext. photos (1939).

Mill House No. 5 (MASS-388), Chestnut St. Frame with clapboarding, one-and-a-half stories, rear ell; built early 19th C. 2 ext. photos (1938, 1939).

Mill Houses (MASS-388), Chestnut St. & Sullivan Ave.

Frame with clapboarding, one-and-a-half stories; built early 19th C. 1 ext. photo (1938, includes three houses).

St. Mary's Episcopal Church (MASS-389). Frame with clapboarding and matched siding, 1 story with square two-stage tower; built early 19th C. 4 ext. photos (1937), 5 int. photos (1939).

Woodward, John, House (MASS-146), 268 Woodward St. Frame with clapboarding, two stories, rear wings; built c. 1700. 11 sheets (1935); 4 ext. photos (1939), 5 int. photos (1939).

Wyman-Tower House (MASS-147), 401 Woodward St. Frame with clapboarding, two stories, hipped roof; built c. 1790. 14 sheets (1935); 2 ext. photos (1930's).

NORTHAMPTON — *Hampshire County*

Allen House (MASS-474). Brick, two stories, square-columned entry porch; built early 19th C. 1 ext. photo (1935), 1 int. photo (1935).

Damon, Isaac, House (MASS-638), 46 Bridge St. Historical house museum. Frame with clapboarding, two stories, rear wing, Doric entry porch; built 1812. Isaac Damon, builder-architect. 3 ext. photos (1959), 2 int. photos (1959); 4 data pages (1959).

Hunt-Brewster House (MASS-644), 18 Old South St. Brick, two stories, Greek Revival details; built c. 1870, two-story frame wing added 1881, late 19th C. alterations. 2 ext. photos (1959), 3 int. photos (1959); 3 data pages (1959).

Parsons, Lieutenant William, House (MASS-188), 392

Bridge St. Frame with clapboarding, two stories; built c. 1744, moved to Darien, Conn., 1937. 17 sheets (1935); 3 data pages (1940).

NORTH ANDOVER — *Essex County*

Barnard, Parson Thomas, House (formerly Governor Simon Bradstreet House) (MASS-2-63), 159 Osgood St. Frame with clapboarding, two stories, rear lean-to; built c. 1715. 12 sheets (1934); 2 ext. photos (1934), 4 int. photos (1934).

Bradstreet, Governor Simon, House (MASS-2-63). See Barnard, Parson Thomas, House (MASS-2-63); North Andover, Mass.

Kittredge, Dr. Thomas, House and Fence (MASS-475), 114 Academy Rd. Frame with clapboarding, three stories, hipped roof with deck balustrade, rear ell; built 1784. Attributed to Samuel McIntire. 3 ext. photos (1940, 1941).

Town Scales House (MASS-2-100), Andover Street. Frame, one story, pyramidal roof; built c. 1819. 1 sheet (1934); 1 ext. photo (1934).

NORTH ATTLEBOROUGH — *Bristol County*

Daggett, Handel, House (MASS-390). Frame with clapboarding, two stories, side wing; built late 18th C. 2 ext. photos (1935), 2 int. photos (1935).

Ellis, Jabez, House (MASS-391). Stone and brick, one story, gambrel roof; built late 18th C. 2 ext. photos (1935), 2 int. photos (1936).

Mann, Dr. Bezaleel, House (MASS-392). Frame with clapboarding, two stories, low hipped roof; built late 18th C. 1 ext. photo (1937), 3 int. photos (1937).

NORTH ATTLEBOROUGH — PLAINVILLE TOWN LINE

Angle Tree Stone (MASS-181), E. of cor. of W. Bacon and Warren Sts. 7'4" high marker with inscription; erected 1790. Marks boundary between Massachusetts Bay Colony and Plymouth Colony. 5 sheets (1935); 2 photos (1935).

NORTH ATTLEBOROUGH VICINITY

Congregational Church (MASS-189), 2 mi. S. of North Attleborough on Old Post Road. Frame with clapboarding, two stories with three-stage tower; built 1828. 23 sheets (1935); 5 ext. photos (1938, including carriage sheds and privies).

Powder House (MASS-148), Mount Hope Avenue, Oldtown. Brick, one story, circular plan, conical roof; built 1768. 1 sheet (1935); 1 ext. photo (1935).

Stanley-Mathewson House (MASS-170), 2.5 mi. from North Attleborough on Old Post Rd. Frame with clapboarding, two stories, rear ell; built before 1829. 8 sheets (1935); 2 ext. photos (1935).

Stearns, Captain John, House (MASS-165), 2 mi. S. of North Attleborough on Old Post Rd. Frame with clapboarding, two stories; built 1740. 12 sheets (1935); 4 ext. photos (1935), 1 int. photo (1935).

NORTH BROOKFIELD — *Worcester County*

Potter, Captain John, House (MASS-852). See West Springfield, Mass.

NORTH CARVER (See CARVER)

NORTH CHATHAM (See CHATHAM)

NORTH DIGHTON (See DIGHTON)

NORTH EASTON (See EASTON)

NORTHFIELD — *Franklin County*

Hall-Spring House (MASS-643), 89 Main St. Frame with clapboarding and matched siding, one-and-a-half stories, 2 Doric porches; built c. 1846. 6 ext. photos (1959); 3 data pages (1959).

Lane, Captain Samuel, House (MASS-661), 33 Main St. Frame with clapboarding, two stories, giant Doric portico, rear ell; built 1845–47. George Stearns, builder-architect. 3 ext. photos (1959), 2 int. photos (1959); 3 data pages (1960).

Mattoon, Isaac, House (MASS-659), 26 Main St. Frame with clapboarding, 2 stories, Doric entry porch, rear ell; built 1801. Calvin Stearns, builder. 5 ext. photos (1959); 3 data pages (1960).

Pomeroy, William, House (MASS-654), W. side Main St., just S. of town center. Frame with clapboarding, two stories, giant Doric portico, rear ell; built c. 1820. Calvin Stearns, builder. 3 ext. photos (1959), 2 int. photos (1959); 3 data pages (1960).

Stratton House (MASS-476). Frame with clapboarding, 2 stories, rear lean-to; built early 18th C. 2 ext. photos (1935).

White-Field House (MASS-655), NE. corner Main and Maple Sts. Frame with clapboarding, 2 stories, hipped roof, rear ell; built 1784, restored early 20th C. 4 ext. photos (1959), 2 int. photos (1959); 3 data pages (1960).

NORTHFIELD VICINITY

Alexander, Simeon, House (MASS-662), 188 Main St., East Northfield. Frame with clapboarding, two stories; built c. 1776, restored. 1 ext. photo (1959), 4 int. photos (1959); 3 data pages (1960).

Colton, Captain Richard, House (MASS-660), E. side Main St., near N. end, East Northfield. Brick painted white, two stories, rear ell; built 1828. 3 ext. photos (1959), 1 int. photo (1959); 2 data pages (1960).

Belding, Elijah E., House (MASS-635), E. side Mt. Hermon Station Rd., N. of road to Northfield, West Northfield. Frame with clapboarding, 2 stories, giant Doric portico, rear wing and shed; built c. 1840. George Stearns, builder. 3 ext. photos (1959), 2 int. photos (1959); 3 data pages (1959).

NORTH PEMBROKE (See PEMBROKE)

NORTH READING — *Middlesex County*

Crosby, Guy M. Jr., House (MASS-523). Frame with clapboarding, 2 stories, gambrel roof; built mid 18th C., later additions and alterations. 2 ext. photos (1941).

NORTH UXBRIDGE — *Worcester County*

Crown and Eagle Mills (MASS-991), 123 Hartford Avenue East. Granite ashlar and brick masonry, 273′ x 44″, three stories, gable roofs (over Crown Mill and Eagle Mill), flat roof (over center connecting mill). Crown (west) Mill and Eagle (east) Mill each have two towers, one on the north and one on the south elevation respectively; north tower of Crown Mill is capped with a bell cupola, the other three towers have gable roofs. Crown Mill built c. 1825, Eagle Mill built c. 1829, Robert Rogerson probable designer; center connecting mill built 1851, Paul Whitin, Jr., probable designer. 7 gen. ext. photos (1967), 6 ext. detail photos (1967), 12 int. photos (1967), 1 photocopy of c. 1840 engraving, 1 photocopy of c. 1855 photo, 1 photocopy of 1877 tapestry (?), 1 photocopy of c. 1940 photo, 1 photocopy of 1907 insurance survey; 6 data pages (1967, 1971).

NORTON — *Bristol County*

Avery, Reverend Joseph, House (MASS-244), Main St. Frame with clapboarding, two stories, rear lean-to; built 1711, later additions and alterations. 7 sheets (1935); 1 ext. photo (1935), 3 int. photos (1935).

Clark, Reverend Pitt, House (MASS-257), Mansfield Ave. Frame with clapboarding, two stories, rear ell; built 1797. 12 sheets (1936); 2 ext. photos (1938), 6 int. photos (1938).

Newcomb, Jonathan, House (MASS-393). Frame with clapboarding, two stories; built early 19th C., later side and rear additions. 4 ext. photos (1937), 3 int. photos (1937).

NORWELL — *Plymouth County*

Bryant-Cushing House (MASS-109), Cornet Stetson Road. Frame with shingles, two stories; built 1698, additions. 12 sheets (1934); 2 ext. photos (1934), 7 int. photos (1934).

OAKHAM — *Worcester County*

Adams, Eli, House (MASS-284). Frame with clapboarding and shingles, two stories, side and rear wings; built 1806, extensive additions and alterations, demolished 1940. 5 ext. photos (1940), 11 int. photos (1940).

Lincoln House (MASS-285). Frame with clapboarding and matched siding, two stories, side wings; built c. 1840, ruinous (1940). 3 ext. photos (1940).

Old Saw Mill (MASS-287). Frame with vertical siding, one story with basement and loft; built mid 19th C., later additions. 7 ext. photos (1940), 2 int. photos (1940).

ORLEANS — *Barnstable County*

Kendrick, Jonathan, House (MASS-119), W. side State Highway, South Orleans. Frame with shingles, one-and-a-half stories; built late 18th C. 6 sheets (1934); 1 ext. photo (1935).

PALMER — *Hampden County*

Boston and Albany Railroad Station (MASS-664). Rough granite, one story, hipped roof; commissioned 1881. Henry Hobson Richardson, architect. 1 ext. photo (1959), 3 int. photos (1959); 3 data pages (1960).

PELHAM — *Hampshire County*

Charcoal Kilns (MASS-2-72), Valley Rd., "Pelham Hollow." Brick, rectangular plan with barrel vault, circular plan with dome; built 1862, demolished. 1 sheet (1934); 3 ext. photos (1934, 1935), 1 photocopy of photo (1900).

PEMBROKE — *Plymouth County*

Society of Friends Meetinghouse (MASS-2-59), corner Schoosett St. and State Rt. 3, North Pembroke. Frame with shingles, two stories, entry wing; built 1706. 7 sheets (1934); 1 ext. photo (1934), 2 int. photos (1934).

PEPPERELL — *Middlesex County*

Jewett, Nehemiah, Bridge (MASS-225), Groton St., over Nashua River. Wooden covered bridge, lattice frame walls, three span; built 1818. 4 sheets (1936); 2 ext. photos (1940).

Prescott, Colonel William, House (MASS-604). Frame with clapboarding, two stories, rear two-story ell and lean-to; built 18th C., later additions and alterations. 2 ext. photos (1941).

PEPPERELL VICINITY

Coburn's Tavern (MASS-226), 2 mi. from Groton Center on South Road (State Rt. 119), South Pepperell. Brick, three stories, two-story end bays; built c. 1790, interior burned 1812. 16 sheets (1937–38).

District School No. 4 (MASS-222), corner North and Prescott Streets, North Pepperell. Brick, one story, one room; probably built early 19th C., additions c. 1840. 3 sheets (1936).

PITTSFIELD — *Berkshire County*

"Arrowhead" (Bush-Melville House) (MASS-2-23), Holmes Rd., about 1 mi. from Pomeroy Ave. Frame with clapboarding, 2 stories, rear two-story wing; built 1794. Originally a tavern; later owned by author Herman Melville. 3 sheets (1934); 2 ext. photos (1934), 1 int. photo (1934).

Brattle, William Jr., House (MASS-2-54), 626 Williams St. Frame with clapboarding, two stories, gambrel roof; built 1762. 6 sheets (1934); 1 ext. photo (1934), 3 int. photos (1934).

Bulfinch Church (MASS-2-24), corner North St. and Maple Ave. Frame with clapboarding, 2 stories (originally one story and balcony) with tower; built 1789–93, moved from Park Row and North St., demolished after 1934. Charles Bulfinch, architect. 11 sheets (1934); 4 ext. photos (1934), 2 int. photos (1934).

Colt-Pingree House (MASS-477). Brick, two stories, Ionic tetrastyle portico; built early 19th C. 1 ext. photo (1935).

First Bank Building (MASS-2-46), 800 East St. Frame with clapboarding and matched siding, two stories; built 1806, moved to present site 1874, altered. 1 sheet (1934); 1 ext. photo (1934).

Peace Party House (MASS-478), SE. corner East St. and Wendell Ave. Frame with clapboarding, two-and-a-half stories, rear wing; built mid 18th C. 1 ext. photo (1935).

West Part School (MASS-2-89), corner West and Churchill Sts. Frame with clapboarding, one story; built early 19th C. 1 sheet (1934); 1 ext. photo (1935).

PITTSFIELD VICINITY (See HANCOCK)

PLAINVILLE — *Norfolk County*

Slack, Benjamin, House (MASS-155), South St. at town center. Frame with clapboarding, 2 stories, clear-story; built early 18th C. 7 sheets (1935); 1 ext. photo (1935).

PLYMOUTH — *Plymouth County*

Warren, David, House Garden (MASS-185), 24 North Street. Center-path garden; laid out before 1839 (house built 1803). 2 sheets (1936).

PRESCOTT — *Worcester County (Flooded as part of Quabbin Reservoir, 1938)*

Red School House (MASS-193), on road to Cooleyville. Frame with clapboarding, one story; built early 19th C., demolished 1937. 2 sheets (1936); 2 ext. photos (1935).

School House (MASS-2-98), road to Enfield. Frame with clapboards, one story; built 1813, demolished 1937. 2 sheets (1934); 1 ext. photo (1934).

PROVINCETOWN — *Barnstable County*

Church of the Redeemer (Universalist) (MASS-737), Commercial Street. Frame with clapboarding, three-stage tower, Greek Revival; built 1847. 3 ext. photos (1962*), 3 int. photos (1962*); 1 data page (1962*).

Pilgrim Monument (MASS-738), off Bradford St. Granite ashlar, rectangular shaft, 255' high, crenelated; built 1907–10. 1 ext. photo (1959*).

Quincy — *Norfolk County*

Adams, John, Birthplace (MASS-596), 133 Franklin St. Museum. Frame with clapboarding, 2 stories, rear lean-to and wing; built early 18th C. 1 ext. photo (1941).

Adams, John Quincy, Birthplace (MASS-597), 141 Franklin St. Museum. Frame with clapboarding, two stories, rear lean-to; built 1716. 1 ext. photo (1941).

Adams Mansion and Garden (MASS-215, 615), 135 Adams St., Adams National Historic Site. Museum. Frame with clapboarding, brick, two-and-a-half stories with gambrel roof; built 1731 by Major Leonard Vassall, remodeled by Adams family often since purchase in 1787, given to Government 1946. 38 sheets (1935, 1936, a garden survey, MASS-215; 1956, MASS-615); 4 ext. photos (1954), 1 int. photo (1954*), 3 photocopies of watercolor and drawings (1798*, 1822*, 1844*); 7 data pages (1958).

Adams Mansion Library (MASS-841), 135 Adams Street, Adams National Historic Site. Brick and ashlar, one story, one-room plan; built 1870. Edward C. Cabot, architect. 2 sheets (1956*); 1 ext. photo (1954*), 1 int. photo (1954*).

Adams Mansion Woodshed (MASS-842), 135 Adams Street by Newport Ave., Adams National Historic Site. Frame with vertical and horizontal wood siding, one story; built 1799, moved to present location in 1870's. 3 sheets (1956*).

102

Granite Railway (MASS-150), from Pine Hill Quarry to Neponset River. Built in 1826 to convey granite in horse-drawn wagons for Bunker Hill Monument. Gridley J. F. Bryant, designer and builder. 6 sheets (1934); 9 ext. photos (1934, 1940, including now destroyed railroad house).

Quincy, Colonel Josiah, House (MASS-2-42), 20 Muirhead Street. Frame with clapboarding, two stories with monitor; built 1770. 13 sheets (1934); 4 ext. photos (1934), 4 int. photos (1934).

Stone Temple ("Church of the Presidents") (MASS-599), 1266 Hancock St. Coursed ashlar, giant Doric portico, tower; built 1828, cupola added later. Alexander Parris, architect. John and John Quincy Adams worshiped and are buried here. 2 ext. photos (1941).

READING — *Middlesex County*

Parker Tavern (Abram Bryant, Jr., House) (MASS-522), Washington St. near State Rt. 28. Frame with clapboarding and shingles, two stories, rear lean-to; nucleus built 1694, later additions and alterations, restored 1929. 2 ext. photos (1941).

REHOBOTH — *Bristol County*

Carpenter, Colonel Thomas, House (MASS-394). Frame with clapboarding, two stories, two-story side wing; built late 18th C. 2 ext. photos (1936), 2 int. photos (1936).

REVERE VICINITY

Bennett, Samuel, House ("Rumney Hall") (MASS-218), 50 Marshall St., Franklin Park. Frame with clapboard-

ing and shingles, two stories; built early 18th C.
Demolished by 1965. 11 sheets (1935).

Bennett-Slade-Parsons House (MASS-218). See Bennett, Samuel, House (MASS-218); Revere Vicinity, Mass.

RICHMOND — *Berkshire County*

Peirson House (MASS-396). Frame with clapboarding, two stories; built late 18th C. 2 ext. photos (1935), 1 ext. photo of gazebo (1935).

RIVERSIDE (See GILL)

ROCKPORT — *Essex County*

Bradley's Wharf (MASS-227), Bearskin Neck. Frame with vertical siding, one story; built before 1880. 2 sheets (1938).

ROWLEY — *Essex County*

Billings House and Fence (MASS-277), Main St. Frame with clapboarding, 2 stories, side wing; wooden picket fence, square posts, urns; house built c. 1830, fence c. 1840. 3 sheets (1937, 1938); 2 ext. photos (1940).

ROXBURY (See BOSTON)

RUTLAND — *Worcester County*

Putnam, General Rufus, House (MASS-2-71), Main St. Frame with clapboarding, two stories, hipped roof; built c. 1750. 15 sheets (1934); 3 ext. photos (1934), 4 int. photos (1934).

Andrew, John, House and Garden (MASS-281A), 13 Washington Sq. Brick, three stories with deck balustrade, giant order side porch; small formal garden; built and laid out 1818. 4 sheets (1938); 6 ext. photos (1940).

Andrew, John, Stable (MASS-281), 13 Washington Square. Brick, two stories, plain pilasters & recessed window panels; built 1818. 6 sheets (1940); 2 ext. photos (1940).

Baldwin-Lyman Fence (MASS-485), 92 Washington Sq. Square wooden posts and pickets with caps and urn finials; built 1818. 3 photos (1939).

Boardman-Bowen Fence (MASS-490), 1 Boardman Street. Square wooden posts and pickets with caps and urn finials, arched gate; built late 18th C. 2 photos (1938).

Brooks House (MASS-796), 260 Lafayette St. at Laurel. Frame with rusticated wooden siding, two stories, Gothic details; 1 ext. photo (1958*); 1 data page (1958*).

Cook-Oliver House (MASS-333), 142 Federal St. Frame with clapboarding, 3 stories, hipped roof; built 1802–03. Samuel McIntire, architect. Fine details. 7 ext. photos (1938), 16 int. photos (1939), 2 photocopies of views (c. 1900).

Corwin, Jonathan, House ("The Old Witch House") (MASS-398), 310 Essex St. Historic house museum. Frame with clapboarding, two stories with overhang; built 1675. 2 ext. photos (1940).

Crombie, Benjamin, House Garden (Joel Bowker Garden) (MASS-262), 9 Crombie St. Semiformal garden; laid out 1824. 2 sheets (1938).

Crowninshield-Devereux House (MASS-582), 74 Washington Sq. Frame with clapboarding, three stories, hipped roof with balustrade; built c. 1804–06. Samuel McIntire, architect. 2 ext. photos (1941).

Crowninshield Warehouse (MASS-259), India St. Brick, three stories, hipped roof; built c. 1810. 4 sheets (1938); 2 ext. photos (1938).

Custom House and Public Stores (MASS-799), 178 Derby St., Salem Maritime National Historic Site. Brick, two stories on high basement, hipped roof with balustrade, composite order entry porch, rear three-story warehouse wing; built 1818–19, additions and alterations 1853–54. 17 sheets (1958*); 7 ext. photos (1958*), 7 int. photos (1958*); 1 photocopy of old plot plan (n.d.*); 2 data pages (1958*).

Custom House Scale House (MASS-800), Orange St., Custom House yard, Salem Maritime National Historic Site. Brick, one story, one-room plan; built 1829. 2 sheets (1958*); 1 ext. photo (1958*); 6 data pages (1958*).

Daland, Benjamin, House Garden (John Robinson Garden) (MASS-208A), 18 Summer Street. Central path with irregular beds of flowers and shrubs; laid out 1851. By "Weeks, a Scotish gardener." 3 sheets (1936).

Daland, Benjamin, House Stable (John Robinson Stable) (MASS-208), 18 Summer St. Frame with clapboarding, two stories, decorative wooden panels with swags

106

(Samuel McIntire); built before 1825. 8 sheets (1936); 3 ext. photos (1940).

Daniel, Stephen, House (MASS-116), corner Daniels and Essex Streets. Frame with clapboarding, three stories, rear lean-to and ell; built 1693. 16 sheets (1934); 3 ext. photos (1934, 1937), 9 int. photos (1934, 1936).

Derby, Richard, House (MASS-269), 168 Derby Street, Salem Maritime National Historic Site. Brick, two-and-a-half stories, gambrel roof; built 1761–62, kitchen ell 1811, restored 1928, 1938. Home of early merchant family. Fine interiors. 5 sheets (1962*); 7 ext. photos (1940, 1958*), 8 int. photos (1958*); 17 data pages (1958*).

Dodge, Pickering, House and Garden (MASS-184), 40 Dearborn Street at North River waterfront. Frame with clapboarding, two-and-a-half stories, Doric portico; semiformal axial garden; built and laid out 1837. 4 sheets (1935, 1936); 4 ext. photos (1940, including gazebo).

Dodge-Shreve House (MASS-795), 29 Chestnut St. Brick, three stories, hipped roof with deck balustrade; built early 19th C. 2 ext. photos (1958*); 1 data page (1958*).

East India Marine Hall (Peabody Museum) (MASS-798), 161 Essex St. Brick, 2 stories; built 1824, later additions and alterations. 2 ext. photos (1958*), 1 int. photo (1958*), 1 photocopy of old ext. photo (n.d.*), 3 photocopies of original measured drawings (c. 1824*); 1 data page (1958*).

Finnegan, Doctor, Fence (MASS-487). Detail of wooden

107

post with cap and fluted urn; built early 19th C. 1 photo (1938).

First Universalist Meetinghouse (MASS-399). Brick, two stories with square entry tower; built 1808. 2 ext. photos (1936), 6 int. photos (1936).

Forrester-Peabody House and Garden (MASS-264), 29 Washington Square. Brick, three stories with deck balustrade; center-path garden; built and laid out 1818. 3 sheets (1938); 4 ext. photos (1940, 1941).

Forrester's Warehouse (MASS-572), 187 Derby Street, Central Wharf, Salem Maritime National Historic Site. Brick, three stories, hipped roof; built before 1832, extensively altered, fire damage 1914, demolished 1948. 4 sheets (1941).

Gardner-White-Pingree House and Garden (MASS-271), 128 Essex St. Historic house museum. Brick, three stories with balustrade, Corinthian entry porch; built 1804–05, garden altered 1938. Samuel McIntire, architect. 1 sheet (1938); 2 ext. photos (1940).

Hamilton Hall (MASS-483), 7 Cambridge Street at Chestnut. Brick, three stories, recessed window panels; built 1805–24, later additions. Samuel McIntire, architect. 2 ext. photos (1940), 1 photocopy of original plans (c. 1805*).

Hawkes, General Benjamin, House (MASS-270), 4 Custom House Place, Salem Maritime National Historic Site. Frame with clapboarding, three stories with deck balustrade; built 1801. Samuel McIntire, architect. 3 ext. photos (1937, 1940), 9 int. photos (1937, 1938), 3 photocopies of original plan and elevations (c. 1801*).

108

Hawthorne, Nathaniel, Birthplace (MASS-581), 27 Union St. Frame with clapboarding, 2 stories, gambrel roof; mid 18th C. around late 17th C. nucleus, later additions and alterations. 1 ext. photo (1941).

Hodges, Captain Jonathan, Garden House (MASS-265), 12 Chestnut St. Frame with diagonal lattice walls, ogee roof; built c. 1845. 1 sheet (1938); 1 ext. photo (1940).

Hodges-Webb-Meek House (MASS-797), 81 Essex Street at Orange. Frame with clapboarding, two-and-a-half stories, gambrel roof; built early 19th C. 2 ext. photos (1962*), 2 int. photos (1962*).

"House of the Seven Gables" (John Turner House) (MASS-629), 54 Turner St. Museum. Frame with clapboarding, two-and-a-half stories with overhang; nucleus built c. 1668, later additions and alterations, restored 1910. Made famous by Nathaniel Hawthorne's book. 1 ext. photo (1935).

Lindall-Barnard-Andrews Fence (MASS-484), 393 Essex St. Wooden posts with fluted pilasters and urn, round pickets; built early 19th C. 2 photos (1938).

Lindall-Gibbs-Osgood Garden (MASS-263), 314 Essex St. Irregular plan, wooden carriage gates; laid out c. 1837. 2 sheets (1938).

Loring-Emmerton House (MASS-480), Essex St. Brick, three stories with deck balustrade; built early 19th C., remodeled. 6 ext. photos (1938, 1940, including fence details).

Manning, Robert, Garden (MASS-187), 33 Dearborn St. Informal, central-path garden; laid out 1825. One of first "pomological gardens" in the country. 4 sheets (1935).

Narbonne House (MASS-802), 71 Essex St. Frame with clapboarding, two stories, gable and shed roofs; built c. 1671, later rear and side additions. 4 sheets (1962*); 6 ext. photos (1958*, 1961*, 1962*, including barn), 9 int. photos (1962*, including barn), 6 photocopies of ext. photos (c. 1884*, 1891*, 1900*, n.d.*), 3 photocopies of int. photos (1888*, 1891*); 28 data pages (1962*).

Oliver Primary School (MASS-329). Brick, two stories, hipped roof, pilasters and recessed window panels; built early 19th C. 4 ext. photos (1936, 1940); 1 photocopy of print (c. 1900).

Peabody Museum (MASS-798). See East India Marine Hall (MASS-798); Salem, Mass.

Phillips House and Fence (MASS-488), 36 Chestnut St. Frame with clapboarding, 3 stories, hipped roof, Ionic porch; built early 19th C. 4 ext. photos (1940, including 2 fence details).

Phippen, Doctor, House and Fence (MASS-486), Chestnut St. Frame with matched siding, two stories with pilasters, hipped roof; built early 19th C. 3 ext. photos (1938, including two fence details).

Pickering House (MASS-482), 30 Chestnut St. Frame with clapboarding and giant pilasters, three stories, hipped roof with deck balustrade. 1 ext. photo (1940).

Pickering, John, House and Garden (MASS-212), 18 Broad St. Frame with matched siding and clapboarding, two stories; built 1660, Gothic details added 1841, informal garden laid out 1841. 6 sheets (1935, garden details only); 1 ext. photo (1940).

Pickman, Benjamin, House (MASS-332), 165 Essex St. Frame with clapboarding, two-and-a-half stories, gambrel roof; built 1750, remodeled c. 1800, demolished 1941. 4 ext. photos (1940), 3 int. photos (1940).

Pierce, Jerathmeel, House and Garden (Pierce-Nichols House) (MASS-224), 80 Federal St. Historic house museum. Frame with clapboarding, three stories with deck balustrade; central-path garden; built 1782, laid out 1782. Attributed to Samuel McIntire, architect. 9 sheets (1936, 1937); 7 ext. photos (1940).

Robinson, John, Garden (MASS-208A). See Daland, Benjamin, House Garden (MASS-208A); Salem, Mass.

Robinson, John, Stable (MASS-208). See Daland, Benjamin, House Stable (MASS-208); Salem, Mass.

Ropes Memorial (MASS-481), 318 Essex St. Museum. Frame with clapboarding, two-and-a-half stories, gambrel roof; built 1719, later additions, restored. 1 ext. photo (1941).

Rum Shop (MASS-801), NW. corner Derby St. and Palfrey Court, Salem Maritime National Historic Site. Frame with clapboarding, two stories; built early 19th C. 2 sheets (1958*); 1 ext. photo (1958*); 1 data page (1958*).

Saunders, Thomas, Garden (Leverett Saltonstall Garden) (MASS-228), 41 Chestnut St. Semiformal central-path garden behind one section of 1808 double brick house; laid out 1808. 4 sheets (1937); 2 photos (1940).

Ship Chandler's Shop (MASS-291), corner Federal and North Streets. Frame with clapboarding, two-and-a-half stories, two-story rear ell; built c. 1799. 7 sheets (1938, 1940); 2 ext. photos (1940).

Turner, John, House (MASS-629). See "House of the Seven Gables" (MASS-629); Salem, Mass.

Ward, Joshua, House ("Washington House") (MASS-2-57), 148 Washington St. Brick, three stories, hipped roof; built c. 1760, altered. 11 sheets (1934); 4 ext. photos (1937), 15 int. photos (1937).

Waters-Bertram House (Public Library) (MASS-803), 370 Essex St. Brick, three stories, hipped roof with deck balustrade; built 1818, later additions and alterations. 2 ext. photos (1958*); 1 data sheet (1958*).

SANDWICH — *Barnstable County*

Hoxie House (MASS-739), S. side of Rt. 130, near Shawme Lake. Frame with vertical siding, two stories; built c. 1720, restored 1959. Reputedly the oldest house on Cape Cod. 2 ext. photos (1959*); 2 data pages (1960*).

Nye House (MASS-206), S. of King's Highway on Old County Rd., East Sandwich. Frame with shingles, two stories; built mid 18th C. 2 sheets (1935); 1 ext. photo (1935).

SAUGUS — *Essex County*

"Scotch" Boardman House (MASS-492), Howard St. Frame with clapboarding and shingles, two stories with overhang, rear lean-to; built c. 1686. Housed Scottish

112

prisoners who worked in local ironworks. 1 sheet (1945, plans only); 2 ext. photos (1940).

SCITUATE — *Plymouth County*

"Old Oaken Bucket" House (MASS-2-41), Old Oaken Bucket Rd., Greenbush, 1.75 mi. from Scituate. Frame with shingles, one story; built 1835. 6 sheets (1934); 2 ext. photos (1934).

Stedman, Isaac, Grist Mill (MASS-2-14), Country Way, Greenbush. Frame with shingles, one story on high basement; built 1640. 3 sheets (1934); 1 ext. photo (1934), 1 int. photo (1934).

Lighthouse and Keeper's House (MASS-2-22), Cedar Point, Scituate Harbor. Ashlar and brick tower; frame with shingle house, connecting wings; built 1810. 5 sheets (1934); 2 ext. photos (1934).

SEEKONK — *Bristol County*

Martin, Lieutenant-Governor Simeon, Blacksmith Shop (MASS-235), County St. Frame with clapboarding and shingles, one story and loft; built c. 1765. 4 sheets (1940).

Martin, Lieutenant-Governor Simeon, House (MASS-2-90), County Street. Frame with clapboarding, two-and-a-half stories, monitor; built 1810. 20 sheets (1934); 3 ext. photos (1935), 3 int. photos (1935).

Martin, Sylvanus, Barn (MASS-234), County St. Frame with shingles, one story; built c. 1760, destroyed 1938. 3 sheets (1937).

SHARON — *Norfolk County*

Cobb's Tavern (MASS-336), 36 Bay St. Frame with clapboarding, brick end walls, two stories; built late 18th C. 4 ext. photos (1936, 1938), 5 int. photos (1938); 16 data pages (1955).

SHEFFIELD — *Berkshire County*

Ashley, Colonel John, House (MASS-401), off Cooper Rd. Frame with clapboarding, 2 stories; built mid 18th C. 3 ext. photos (1935), 6 int. photos (1935).

Ashley, General John, House (MASS-400). Frame with clapboarding, two stories; built early 19th C. 1 ext. photo (1937, doorway detail).

Congregational Church (MASS-892). Frame with clapboarding, two stories with three-stage tower and spire; built 1760, remodeled 1819. "Sheffield Declaration" adopted here in 1773. 2 ext. photos (1930's*).

Hall, Parker L., Law Office (MASS-233), State Rt. 7. Frame with clapboarding, one story; built c. 1826. 1 sheet (1935); 1 ext. photo (1935).

SHELBURNE — *Franklin County*

Arms House (MASS-493), on Shelburne-Colrain Rd. Brick, two stories, rear ell; built late 18th C. 2 ext. photos (1935).

Bardwell, Daniel P., House (MASS-657), E. side Bardwell's Ferry Rd., 2¾ mi. S. of Shelburne Center. Frame with clapboarding, two stories, one-story rear and side wings; built 1842 or 1843 (ell part of earlier house). 4

114

ext. photos (1959), 6 int. photos (1959); 4 data pages (1960).

Bardwell, Daniel P., Ash House (MASS-691), East side Bardwell's Ferry Rd., 2¾ mi. S. of Shelburne Center. Brick, one story, gable roof. 1 ext. photo (1959).

SHERBORN — *Middlesex County*

Leland, Deacon William, House (MASS-402). Frame with clapboarding, 2 stories with one-story side wing; built early 18th C. 4 ext. photos (1941).

SHIRLEY — *Middlesex County*

First Parish Meetinghouse (MASS-540). Frame with clapboarding, 2 stories, three-stage tower; built 1773, porch added 1804, remodeled 1839. 4 ext. photos (1941, including 2 views of mid 19th C. fence).

Shirley Shakers' Meetinghouse (MASS-724). Moved 1962 to Hancock Shaker Community, Hancock, Mass. See Hancock Shakers' Meetinghouse (MASS-724); Hancock, Mass.

Stone Pound (MASS-541). Rectangular fieldstone enclosure, surrounded by granite posts and iron rails; built 19th C. 2 photos (1941).

SIASCONSET (See NANTUCKET)

SOMERSET — *Bristol County*

Bowers, Jarathmael, House (MASS-2-17), 55 Main St. Frame with clapboarding and imitation ashlar, two-and-a-half stories, gambrel roof, rear ell; built 1770, later additions, demolished by 1965. 21 sheets (1934); 3 ext. photos (1934), 5 int. photos (1934).

Brayton, John, Homestead (MASS-2-43), Brayton Ave. Frame with clapboarding, two stories, rear ell; built 1796. 9 sheets (1934); 1 ext. photo (1934), 1 int. photo (1934).

Pettis, Henry, House (MASS-2-52), corner Main St. and Pierce Road. Frame with clapboarding, two stories; built c. 1800, partly demolished and altered 1934. 10 sheets (1934), 2 ext. photos (1934).

SOMERVILLE — *Middlesex County*

Powder House (MASS-178), corner Broadway and College Ave., Nathan Tufts Park. Fieldstone, circular plan, conical roof; built c. 1710 as windmill. 1 sheet (1936); 2 ext. photos (1935).

Round Barn (MASS-501). Frame with clapboarding, three stories, circular plan, Ionic doorway; built mid 19th C. 3 ext. photos (1941).

Tufts, Francis, House (MASS-403). Frame with clapboarding, two-and-a-half stories, gambrel roof; built mid 18th C., later additions and alterations. 1 ext. photo (1935), 2 int. photos (1935).

Tufts, Oliver, House (MASS-404), 78 Sycamore St. Frame with clapboarding, 2 stories, gambrel roof; built mid 18th C., later additions and alterations, moved to present site. Headquarters of Major General Lee during Revolutionary siege of Boston. 1 ext. photo (1936).

116

SOUTH BOSTON (See BOSTON)

SOUTH EGREMONT (See EGREMONT)

SOUTH HINGHAM (See HINGHAM)

SOUTH LEE (See LEE)

SOUTH ORLEANS (See ORLEANS)

SOUTH SUDBURY (See SUDBURY)

SOUTH WILLIAMSTOWN (See WILLIAMS-TOWN)

SPRINGFIELD — *Hampden County*

Alexander House (MASS-406). Frame with matched siding and clapboarding, two stories with parapet, giant Corinthian portico, rear ell; built 1811. 6 ext. photos (1938), 10 int. photos (1938), 1 photocopy of photo (c. 1900).

Boston Road Stone (MASS-407). Carved marker; 1763. Erected by Joseph Wait. 1 photo (1937).

Church of the Unity (MASS-637), 207 State St. Ashlar, basilican plan, corner tower with spire, Gothic Revival; built 1867. Henry Hobson Richardson, architect. 3 ext. photos (1959), 3 int. photos (1959); 8 data pages (1959, 1961).

STOCKBRIDGE — *Berkshire County*

Congregational Church (MASS-894), on the Common. Brick, two stories with wooden three-stage tower and spire; built 1824. Ralph Bigelow, builder. 1 ext. photo (1930's*).

Hopkins, Mark, House (MASS-408). Frame with clapboarding, one-and-a-half stories, gambrel roof; built early 18th C. 1 ext. photo (1935).

Housatonic National Bank (MASS-895), Brick, 1 story with Doric portico: built early to mid 19th C. 1 ext. photo (1930's*).

Yale-Duryea Walter Mills (MASS-107), E. Main Street. Frame with clapboarding, one-and-a-half stories, grist, planing, and saw mill; built c. 1823. 2 sheets (1934, 1935); 6 ext. photos (1934).

STONEHAM — *Middlesex County*

First Congregational Church (MASS-593). Frame with clapboarding, matched siding, and pilasters, one story with tower and spire; built mid 19th C. 1 ext. photo (1941).

Green, Jonathan, House (MASS-527). Frame with clapboarding, two stories, rear ell; built 1720. 1 ext. photo (1941).

STOUGHTON — *Norfolk County*

Atherton, Samuel, House (MASS-200), 449 Central St. Frame with clapboarding, two stories, hipped roof, rear ell; built 1812. 7 sheets (1935); 2 ext. photos (1935).

Washington Hotel (MASS-171), 710 Turnpike St. Brick, two stories, hipped roof, frame ell; built 1808. 10 sheets (1935); 3 ext. photos (1940), 2 int. photos (1940).

118

STURBRIDGE — *Worcester County*

Towne, General Salem, House (MASS-2-38), Old Sturbridge Village. Frame with clapboarding, two stories, hipped roof with monitor, rear wings; built 1796. Moved from Old Country Rd., Charlton Center by 1965. 16 sheets (1934); 3 ext. photos (1934), 5 int. photos (1934).

Wright, Oliver, House (MASS-217), State Rt. 131. Frame with clapboarding, two-and-a-half stories, hip-gambrel roof; built 1783. 15 sheets (1936, 1937); 3 ext. photos (1937), 2 int. photos (1937).

SUDBURY — *Middlesex County*

Wayside Inn (Howe's or Red Horse Tavern) (MASS-632), Old Boston Post Road (U.S. Rt. 20), South Sudbury. Museum. Frame with clapboarding, two-and-a-half stories with overhang, gambrel roof; nucleus built c. 1686, later additions and alterations, largely destroyed by fire 1955, restored 1958. Made famous by Longfellow. 2 ext. photos (c. 1935).

SWAMPSCOTT — *Essex County*

Humphrey, John, House (MASS-580), 99 Paradise Rd. Frame with clapboarding and shingles, two-and-a-half stories with overhang, rear lean-to; late 17th C., later additions and alterations. 1 ext. photo (1941).

SWANSEA — *Bristol County*

Luther, Joseph G., Store (MASS-134), Luther's Corner. Brick, two stories, rear lean-to; built c. 1810. 3 sheets (1935); 4 ext. photos (1935), 4 int. photos (1935).

Old Tavern (MASS-105), N. of GAR Highway (U.S. Rt. 6) and Medford Rd., just W. of Cole River. Brick and frame with shingles, two stories, hipped roof; built c. 1770. 11 sheets (1934); 2 ext. photos (1934).

TAUNTON — *Bristol County*

Dean, Nathan, House (MASS-143), Old Colony Road, East Taunton. Frame with clapboarding and shingles, brick end walls, two stories, hipped and gable roofs; built 1724, enlarged 1810. 16 sheets (1934, 1935); 7 ext. photos (1935, including 1 of privy), 5 int. photos (1935).

TEMPLETON — *Worcester County*

Federated Church (MASS-848). See First Parish Congregational Church (MASS-848); Templeton, Mass.

First Parish Congregational Church (Federated Church) (MASS-848), S. side of the Common. Frame with clapboarding, 2 stories with four-stage tower and spire; built 1811. Elias Carter, builder. 2 ext. photos (1940*).

Lee, Colonel Artemus, House (MASS-849), E. side of Common. Frame with clapboarding, 2 stories, giant tetrastyle Tuscan portico, extensive rear wing; built 1829, later alterations. 1 ext. photo (1940*).

Stiles, John W., House (MASS-847), N. side of the Common. Museum. Brick, two stories, hipped roof, side wing; built c. 1810. 1 ext. photo (1940*).

TISBURY — *Dukes County*

Gray, Lucy, House (MASS-2-88), Indian Hill Rd. Frame with shingles, one-and-a-half stories, rear and side ells; built c. 1790. 4 sheets (1934); 3 ext. photos (1935).

TOPSFIELD — *Essex County*

Andrews House (MASS-621). Frame with clapboarding, 2 stories, rear lean-to; built c. 1710, later additions. 3 sheets (1945).

Capen, Parson Joseph, House (MASS-214), Howlett St. just off village common. Frame with clapboarding and shingles, 2 stories with overhang, rear ell; built 1683, restored 1915. An outstanding 17th C. New England home. 6 ext. photos (1935, 1936); 1 data page (1930's).

Elmwood Mansion (MASS-524). Frame with clapboarding and matched siding, brick end walls, three stories, hipped roof; built early 19th C. 2 ext. photos (1941).

TOWNSEND — *Middlesex County*

Conant House (MASS-536). Frame with clapboarding, 2 stories, hipped roof, side and rear wings; built c. 1735, later additions and alterations. 3 ext. photos (1941).

Methodist Episcopal Church (MASS-533). Frame with clapboarding, 2 stories, entry tower with two octagonal stages; built early 19th C. 3 ext. photos (1941).

Spaulding Cooperage Shop (MASS-535). Frame with clapboarding, one-and-a-half stories, rear lean-to; built c. 1845, later additions and alterations, restored, 2 ext. photos (1941).

Spaulding Grist Mill (MASS-534). Museum. Frame with matched siding (original section) and clapboarding and shingles, one-and-a-half stories; built c. 1840, later additions. 2 ext. photos (1941).

TRURO — *Barnstable County*

Adams, Zenas, House (MASS-740), S. side North Pamet Rd. Frame with shingles and clapboarding, one-and-a-half stories; built mid 19th C. 3 ext. photos (1962*), 2 int. photos (1962*); 4 data pages (1962*).

Atkins, Jonah, House (MASS-707), N. side South Pamet Rd. Frame with shingles and clapboarding, one-and-a-half stories; built early 19th C. 3 sheets (1960*); 3 ext. photos (1960*), 3 int. photos (1960*); 5 data pages (1960*).

Cobb, Elisha, House (MASS-705), S. side Prince Valley Rd. Frame with shingles and clapboarding, one-and-a-half stories; built early 19th C. 3 sheets (1962*); 2 ext. photos (1962*, 1963*), 1 int. photo (1962*); 6 data pages (1962*).

Cobb, Elisha, Summer Kitchen (MASS-706), S. side Prince Valley Road. Frame with vertical siding, one story; built early 19th C. 1 sheet (1962*); 1 ext. photo (1962*); 2 data pages (1962*).

Cole, Joseph S., House (MASS-741), N. side Prince Valley Rd., E. of Old County Rd. Frame with shingles and clapboarding, one-and-a-half stories; built before 1850. 1 ext. photo (1959*); 4 data pages (1959*).

Collins, Benjamin, House (MASS-711), N. side South Pamet Road. Frame with shingles, one-and-a-half stories; built early or mid 18th C. 4 sheets (1960*); 3 ext. photos (1960*); 5 data pages (1960*).

Collins, Jonathan, House (MASS-742), S. side South Pamet Rd., 2/3 mi. E. of U.S. Rt. 6. Frame with

122

shingles, one-and-a-half stories; built early 19th C. 2 ext. photos (1962*), 1 photocopy of view (c. 1900*); 6 data pages (1962*).

Dyer, Benjamin, House (MASS-743), S. side North Pamet Rd., 1/2 mi. E. of U.S. Rt. 6. Frame with clapboarding, one-and-a-half stories; built 1834. 2 ext. photos (1962*); 2 data pages (1962*).

Dyer, Benjamin, Barn (MASS-698), S. side North Pamet Rd., 1/2 mi. E. of U.S. Rt. 6. Frame with shingles, one story and loft; built mid 19th C. 2 sheets (1962*); 2 data pages (1962*).

Dyer, Ebenezer, House (MASS-744), S. side Higgins' Hollow Rd., 3/4 mi. E. of U.S. Rt. 6. Frame with shingles and clapboarding, one-and-a-half stories; built late 18th or early 19th C. 2 ext. photos (1960*); 4 data pages (1960*).

Dyer, Joshua, House (MASS-700), N. side North Pamet Rd., about 1 mi. E. of U.S. Rt. 6. Frame with shingles, one-and-a-half stories; built mid 19th C. 3 sheets (1962*); 2 ext. photos (1960*), 1 photocopy of lithograph (c. 1940*); 4 data pages (1960*).

Dyer, Nathaniel, House (MASS-713), N. side North Pamet Rd. Frame with shingles, one-and-a-half stories; built 1830's. 3 sheets (1960*); 3 ext. photos (1960*), 2 int. photos (1960*); 5 data pages (1960*).

Dyer, Thomas, House (MASS-745), S. side Longnook Rd. Frame with clapboarding, one-and-a-half stories; built 1820's. 1 ext. photo (1962*), 2 int. photos (1962*); 6 data pages (1962*).

First Congregational Church (MASS-746), in Truro Center. Frame with clapboarding, square tower; built 1827. 1 ext. photo (1959*), 1 int. photo (1959*); 3 data pages (1957*, 1962*).

Freeman, Edmund, House (MASS-702), Truro Rd. at Ryder Pond, 1/8 mi. W. of U.S. Rt. 6. Frame with shingles, one-and-a-half stories; built 1820's. 5 sheets (1962*); 2 ext. photos (1962*), 2 int. photos (1962*); 5 data pages (1962*).

Freeman, Edmund, Woodhouse (MASS-701), Truro Rd. at Ryder Pond, 1/8 mi. W. of U.S. Rt. 6. Frame with shingles, one story; built early 19th C. 2 sheets (1962*); 1 ext. photo (1962*); 2 data pages (1962*).

Harding, Ephraim, House (MASS-714), N. side South Pamet Road, about 3/4 mi. E. of U.S. Rt. 6. Frame with shingles, one-and-a-half stories; built 1820's. 3 sheets (1960*); 3 ext. photos (1959*, 1960*), 2 int. photos (1960*); 5 data pages (1960*).

Harding, Lot, House (MASS-715). S. side North Pamet Rd., 1¼ mi. E. of Truro Center. Frame with shingles, one-and-a-half stories; built between 1746 and 1782. 5 sheets (1960*); 4 ext. photos (1959*, 1960*), 3 int. photos (1960*); 4 data pages (1960*).

Higgins, Daniel P., House (MASS-747), N. side Higgins' Hollow Rd., near intersection with Longnook Rd. Frame with clapboarding, one-and-a-half stories; built early 19th C. 1 ext. photo (1962*), 3 int. photos (1962*); 4 data pages (1962*).

Higgins, Daniel P., Barn (MASS-696), N. of Higgins' Hollow Road, about 1/3 mi. E. of intersection with

Longnook Road. Frame with plank walls and shingles, one story and loft; built early 19th C. 3 sheets (1962*); 1 ext. photo (1962*), 1 int. photo (1962*); 3 data pages (1962*).

Higgins, Jedediah, House (MASS-748), N. of Higgins' Hollow Rd., 1/3 mi. E. of intersection with Longnook Rd. Frame with clapboarding and shingles, one-and-a-half stories; built early 19th C. 2 ext. photos (1962*), 4 int. photos (1962*); 3 data pages (1962*).

Highland Hotel (MASS-749), NE. of intersection of Old King's Highway and Highland Rd. Frame with clapboarding, two stories; built early 19th C. 1 ext. photo (1959*); 2 data pages (1959*, 1960*).

Highland Lighthouse (MASS-750), Highland Rd. Brick with adjoining brick keeper's house; built 1857. 1 ext. photo (1959*); 3 data pages (1959*).

Hopkins, Thomas, House (MASS-751), at end of Holsbery Lane, 5/8 mi. S. from Old County Rd. Frame with shingles, one-and-a-half stories; built early 19th C. 2 ext. photos (1962*), 2 int. photos (1962*); 4 data pages (1962*).

Kelley, Benjamin S., House (MASS-716), N. side Higgins' Hollow Rd., about 1/2 mi. E. of intersection with Longnook Rd. Frame with clapboarding and shingles, one-and-a-half stories; built c. 1800. 4 sheets (1960*); 3 ext. photos (1960*); 5 data pages (1960*).

Knowles, Paul, House (MASS-752), South Pamet Rd. Frame with clapboarding, one-and-a-half stories; built 1830's. 1 ext. photo (1962*); 1 data page (1962*).

Mayo, Nehemiah, House (MASS-753), 1/2 mi. S. of intersection of Old County and Depot Rds. Frame with shingles, one-and-a-half stories; built c. 1830. 1 ext. photo (1962*), 3 int. photos (1962*); 3 data pages (1962*).

Newcomb, William T., House (MASS-754), Pump Log Point at end of Ryder Beach Rd. Frame with shingles and clapboarding, one-and-a-half stories; built c. 1840. 3 ext. photos (1960*), 3 int. photos (1960*); 5 data pages (1960*).

Paine-Atkins House (MASS-757), S. side Longnook Rd., 1/3 mi. E. of U.S. Rt. 6. Frame with shingles, one-and-a-half stories; built c. 1810–15. 2 ext. photos (1962*), 3 int. photos (1962*), 1 photocopy of view (c. 1890*); 5 data pages (1962*).

Paine, Richard, House (MASS-755), SE. corner intersection of Longnook and Higgins' Hollow Rds. Frame with clapboarding and shingles, one-and-a-half stories; built early 18th C. 3 ext. photos (1960*), 2 int. photos (1960*); 3 data pages (1960*).

Paine, Samuel, House (MASS-756), SE. corner intersection of Longnook and Higgins' Hollow Rds. Frame with clapboarding and shingles, one-and-a-half stories; built early 19th C. 4 ext. photos (1960*), 1 int. photo (1960*); 5 data pages (1960*).

Rich, Atwood, House (MASS-719), N. side Ryder Beach Rd. Frame with clapboarding and shingles, one-and-a-half stories; built early 19th C. 4 sheets (1960*); 2 ext. photos (1960*), 2 int. photos (1960*); 5 data pages (1960*).

Rich, Captain Zoheth, House (MASS-758), N. side Longnook Road at intersection with Higgins' Hollow Rd. Frame with shingles and clapboarding, one-and-a-half stories; built c. 1830. 3 ext. photos (1960*); 4 data pages (1960*, 1962*).

Rich-Cobb House (MASS-766), N. side Prince Valley Road, between Old County Rd. and U.S. Rt. 6. Frame with shingles, one-and-a-half stories; built before 1841. 3 ext. photos (1960*), 3 int. photos (1960*); 3 data pages (1960*).

Rich, Elisha, House (MASS-710), N. side Ryder Beach Rd. Frame with shingles, one-and-a-half stories; built late 18th or early 19th C. 4 sheets (1960*); 3 ext. photos (1960*), 1 int. photo (1960*); 5 data pages (1960*).

Rich, Ephraim, House (MASS-717), Pump Log Point, at end of Ryder Beach Rd. Frame with clapboarding and shingles, one-and-a-half stories; built c. 1830. 3 sheets (1960*); 3 ext. photos (1960*), 5 int. photos (1960*); 5 data pages (1960*).

Rich-Higgins House (MASS-718), S. side Longnook Rd., between Higgins' Hollow Rd. and Longnook Beach. Frame with shingles, one-and-a-half stories; a c. 1830 house joined to a c. 1780 house. 4 sheets (1960*); 5 ext. photos (1960*), 5 int. photos (1960*), 3 photocopies of views (c. 1900*, c. 1905*, 1924*); 6 data pages (1960*).

Rich, Isaac, House (MASS-759), N. side South Pamet Rd., 1/2 mi. E. of U.S. Rt. 6. Frame with clapboarding and shingles, one-and-a-half stories; built mid 19th C. 3 ext. photos (1962*), 1 int. photo (1962*); 3 data pages (1962*).

Rich, Joseph, House (MASS-760), South Pamet Rd. Frame with clapboarding and shingles, one-and-a-half stories; built c. 1826. 3 ext. photos (1962*); 2 data pages (1962*).

Rich, Richard, House (MASS-761), N. side South Pamet Rd., 3/4 mi. from U.S. Rt. 6. Frame with shingles, one-and-a-half stories; built early 19th C. 2 ext. photos (1962*), 3 int. photos (1962*); 3 data pages (1962*).

Rich, Shebnah, House (MASS-764), N. side Longnook Rd., 1 mi. E. of U.S. Rt. 6. Frame with shingles, two stories; built c. 1810, later additions. 1 ext. photo (1962*), 4 int. photos (1962*), 2 photocopies of views (c. 1880*, 1900*); 5 data pages (1962*).

Rich, Thomas, House (MASS-762), E. side Old County Rd., 1½ mi. N. of Wellfleet. Frame with clapboarding, one-and-a-half stories; built c. 1850. 2 ext. photos (1960*), 2 int. photos (1960*); 5 data pages (1960*).

Rich, Thomas Jr., House (MASS-763), W. side Old County Rd. Frame with shingles, one-and-a-half stories; built early 19th C. 3 ext. photos (1960*); 3 data pages (1960*).

Rich, Warren, House (MASS-765), Pump Log Point, at end of Ryder Beach Rd. Frame with clapboarding and shingles, one-and-a-half stories; built c. 1830's. 3 ext. photos (1960*); 2 data pages (1960*).

Small, Isaac, House (MASS-695), W. side intersection Old King's Highway and Highland Rd. Frame with shingles, one-and-a-half stories; built c. 1780. 4 sheets (1962*); 5 ext. photos (1959*, 1962*), 7 int. photos (1962*); 7 data pages (1962*).

Small, Thomas K., House (MASS-767), SW. corner intersection of Highland Rd. and Old King's Highway. Frame with shingles, one-and-a-half stories; built 1820's. 1 ext. photo (1962*); 4 data pages (1962*).

Snow, Ambrose, House and Cobbler Shop (MASS-768), N. side North Pamet Rd., 2/3 mi. from U.S. Rt. 6. Frame with shingles, one-and-a-half stories; built late 18th or early 19th C. 3 ext. photos (1962*), 2 int. photos (1962*); 4 data pages (1962*).

Snow, Ambrose, Privy (MASS-697), N. side North Pamet Rd., 3/4 mi. from U.S. Rt. 6. Frame with shingles; built mid 19th C. 2 sheets (1962*); 1 ext. photo (1962*); 2 data pages (1962*).

Snow, Ephraim, House (MASS-720), S. side North Pamet Rd. Frame with clapboarding, one-and-a-half stories; built c. 1820. 4 sheets (1960*); 3 ext. photos (1960*), 2 int. photos (1960*); 5 data pages (1960*).

Snow, Joshua, House (MASS-769), N. side North Pamet Rd., 1/3 mi. E. of U.S. Rt. 6. Frame with clapboarding and shingles, one-and-a-half stories; built 1820's or 1830's. 4 ext. photos (1962*), 2 int. photos (1962*), 1 photocopy of view (1928*); 4 data pages (1962*).

Snow, Stephen, House (MASS-770), South Pamet Rd. Frame with shingles, one-and-a-half stories; built early 1800's. 3 ext. photos (1962*), 2 int. photos (1962*); 2 data pages (1962*).

Snow, William P., House (MASS-771), South Pamet Rd., 1/3 mi. E. of U.S. Rt. 6. Frame with shingles, one-and-a-half stories; built before 1845. 2 ext. photos

(1962*), 2 int. photos (1962*, 1963*); 3 data pages (1962*).

TYNGSBOROUGH — *Middlesex County*

Brinley-O'Neill House (MASS-409). Frame with clapboarding, three stories with square cupola, two-tiered porch; built late 18th C., later additions. 6 ext. photos (1936, including well house).

School No. 2 (MASS-602). Frame with clapboarding, one story; built early 19th C. 1 ext. photo (1941).

Tyng House (MASS-410). Frame with clapboarding, two-and-a-half stories, gambrel roof, rear additions, giant Ionic portico; built mid 18th C., later additions and alterations. 4 ext. photos (1936), 4 int. photos (1936).

UXBRIDGE — *Worcester County*

Masonic Building and Court House (MASS-411). Brick, two stories; built early 19th C., later alterations. 2 ext. photos (1936), 2 int. photos (1936).

Wheelock, Lieutenant Simeon, House (MASS-412), N. Main St. Frame with clapboarding, one story; built 1768, additions 1789–90, restored 1911. 3 ext. photos (1936), 3 int. photos (1936).

WAKEFIELD — *Middlesex County*

Hartshorne, Colonel James, House (MASS-521), 41 Church St. Frame with clapboarding and shingles, two-and-a-half stories; built mid 18th C., later additions and alterations, restored. 4 ext. photos (1941, including 1 view of 1835 granite water trough).

WALTHAM — *Middlesex County*

Gore, Governor Christopher, Mansion (MASS-210), Gore St., between Main and Grove Streets. Museum. Brick, two-and-a-half stories with elliptical center section, one-and-a-half story wings, balustrades; built c. 1805. 31 sheets (1937–40, including drawings of the coach house and stable, gate, and water pump).

Gore, Governor Christopher, Coach House and Stable (MASS-834), Gore St., between Main and Grove Sts. Frame with clapboarding, two stories; built probably 1805–06, possibly earlier. 3 sheets (MASS-210, sheets 25–27); 7 int. photos (1962*).

Gore, Governor Christopher, Garden (MASS-210A), Gore St. between Main and Grove Sts. General plan of garden (c. 1835) and grounds (1835–46). Robert Murray, an English gardener, was designer. 7 sheets (1936, 1937, including shelter and fences); 2 photos (1940), 1 photocopy of old view (c. 1840).

Stone Mill (MASS-502), South Street. Fieldstone, one story; built early 19th C. 6 ext. photos (1941).

"The Vale" (**Theodore Lyman Garden and Summer House**) (MASS-204), Beaver St. Large estate patterned after Repton; laid out 1793 by Bell, an "English gardener." 15 sheets (1936); 3 ext. photos (1940).

WAREHAM — *Plymouth County*

Fearing, Israel, House (MASS-102), 14 Elm St. Frame with shingles and clapboarding, 2 stories, rear wings; nucleus built 17th C., early and mid 18th C. additions. 16 sheets (1934); 1 ext. photo (1935), 4 int. photos (1935).

WATERTOWN — *Middlesex County*

Bemis, John, House (MASS-131), 425 Main St. Frame with clapboarding, two stories, side and rear wings; built c. 1740. 11 sheets (1934); 2 ext. photos (1935), 1 photocopy of old ext. photo (n.d.).

Brown, Abraham, House (MASS-781), 562 Main St. Museum. Frame with clapboarding and shingles, two stories, built c. 1698. 2 ext. photos (1935).

Caldwell, Daniel, House (MASS-132), 126 Main St. Frame with clapboarding, one-and-a-half stories, gambrel roof, rear lean-to; built c. 1742, demolished 1942. 6 sheets (1934); 2 ext. photos (1935), 2 int. photos (1935).

Conant House (MASS-494). Frame with shingles, two stories, rear lean-to; built 18th C., extensively altered. 2 ext. photos (1935).

WAYLAND — *Middlesex County*

Town Bridge (MASS-2-75), Sudbury Rd., over Sudbury River. Four-arched stone bridge; built 1791. 1 sheet (1934); 1 photo (1935).

WELLESLEY — *Norfolk County*

Boston and Albany Railroad Station (MASS-668). Rough granite ashlar, 1 story, hipped roof; commissioned 1884. Henry Hobson Richardson, architect. Destroyed by 1965. 1 ext. photo (1959), 2 int. photos (1959); 3 data pages (1960, 1961).

Ellis Stone Barn (MASS-145), Boylston St. Rubble

masonry, two stories; built c. 1750. 2 sheets (1934, 1935); 3 ext. photos (1936).

Ware, Ruben, Mill (MASS-546). Fieldstone with ashlar quoins, two-and-a-half stories; built early 19th C., later additions and alterations. 1 ext. photo (1941).

WELLFLEET — *Barnstable County*

Atwood, Ebenezer L., House (MASS-708), S. side Bound Brook Island Rd. Frame with clapboarding and shingles, one-and-a-half stories; built mid 19th C. 2 sheets (1960*); 3 ext. photos (1960*), 3 int. photos (1960*); 5 data pages (1960*).

Atwood, Joel, House (MASS-772), N. side Bound Brook Island Rd. Frame with clapboarding and shingles, one-and-a-half stories; built early 18th C. 1 ext. photo (1962*); 4 data pages (1960*).

Baker, David, House (MASS-709), S. side Bound Brook Rd., about 1 mi. W. of Old County Rd. Frame with clapboarding and shingles, one-and-a-half stories; built early 19th C. 3 sheets (1960*); 3 ext. photos (1959*, 1960*), 2 int. photos (1959*); 7 data pages (1960*).

Freeman, Joseph, House (MASS-773), N. side Old Truro Rd., just N. of Wellfleet Center. Frame with shingles, one-and-a-half stories; built in 1830's. 1 ext. photo (1959*); 3 data pages (1960*).

Gormley, Charles, House (MASS-774), S. side Herring Pond Road, near Herring Pond. Frame with clapboarding and shingles, one-and-a-half stories; built c. 1830. 1 ext. photo (1959); 3 data pages (1960*).

Higgins, Elnathan, House (MASS-775), N. side Pamet Point Rd. Frame with clapboarding and shingles, one-and-a-half stories; built 1830's. 1 ext. photo (1959*); 4 data pages (1959*, 1960*).

Higgins, Josiah, House (MASS-776), between Gull and Higgins' Ponds. Frame with shingles, one-and-a-half stories; built before 1843. 1 ext. photo (1959*); 2 data pages (1960*).

Newcomb, John ("Wellfleet Oysterman"), House (MASS-704), E. side Williams' Pond, about 1/2 mi. N. of Gull Pond Rd. Frame with clapboarding and shingles, one-and-a-half stories; built late 18th C. 2 sheets (1962*); 3 ext. photos (1962*); 5 data pages (1962*).

Rowell House (MASS-777), N. side Gull Pond Rd., about 1 mi. E. of U.S. Rt. 6. Frame with shingles, one-and-a-half stories; built c. 1731. 3 sheets (1960*); 2 ext. photos (1959*); 4 data pages (1960*).

Williams, Justin, House (MASS-703), N. side Pamet Rd., 2/3 mi. W. of U.S. Rt. 6. Frame with clapboarding and shingles, one-and-a-half stories; built early 19th C. 4 sheets (1962*); 3 ext. photos (1962*), 2 int. photos (1962*); 3 data pages (1962*).

Young, B. S., House (MASS-778), E. side U.S. Rt. 6, just N. of Wellfleet Center. Frame with matched boarding and clapboarding, one-and-a-half stories; built after 1843. 1 ext. photo (1959*); 2 data pages (1960*).

WEST BARNSTABLE (See BARNSTABLE)

WEST BROOKFIELD — *Worcester County*

Gilbert, Levi and Peletiah, House (MASS-850). See Gilbert, Levi and Peletiah, House (MASS-850); West Springfield, Mass.

WEST CHATHAM (See CHATHAM)

WESTFIELD — *Hampden County*

Arnold House (MASS-2-35), 140 Franklin St. Frame with clapboarding, two stories, rear wings; built c. 1800, extensive fire damage 1934. 3 sheets (1934); 1 ext. photo (1934).

Fowler, Albert, Tobacco Barn (MASS-103), South St. Extension. Frame with vertical siding, 1 story; built 1855. 1 sheet (1934); 1 ext. photo (1937).

WESTHAMPTON — *Hampshire County*

Hunt, Captain Jared, House (MASS-413). Frame with clapboarding, 2 stories, rear lean-to and wing; built late 18th C. 3 ext. photos (1936, 1937); 1 photocopy of old photo (n.d.).

WEST MEDFORD (See MEDFORD)

WEST NORTHFIELD (See NORTHFIELD)

WESTON — *Middlesex County*

Golden Ball Tavern (MASS-414), 662 Central Avenue. Frame with clapboarding, two stories, hipped roof, rear and side wings; built 1753, later additions. 4 ext. photos (1936), 3 int. photos (1936).

Lamson House (MASS-495). Frame with clapboarding, 2 stories, rear shed wing; built early 19th C. 2 ext. photos (1940).

Lawyer's Office (MASS-2-34), Central Ave. Frame with clapboarding, 1 story, hipped roof; built 1785. 3 sheets (1934); 1 ext. photo (1934).

WESTPORT — *Bristol County*

Waite-Potter House (MASS-2-65), Sanford Rd. Frame with shingles, 1 story; built 1677, enlarged 1760, later alterations, demolished by 1965. 2 sheets (1934); 1 ext. photo (1934).

WESTPORT VICINITY

Richmond-Manchester House (MASS-160), Howland Rd., Acoaxet. Frame with shingles, two stories, rear ell; built 1740. 6 sheets (1935); 1 ext. photo (1935), 1 int. photo (1935).

WEST SPRINGFIELD — *Hampden County*

Atkinson, John, Tavern (MASS-844), Storrowtown, Eastern States Exposition Grounds. Frame with clapboarding, two stories, side wing; built late 18th C., moved from Prescott, Massachusetts. 3 int. photos (1940*).

Chesterfield Blacksmith Shop (NH-41), Storrowton, Eastern States Exposition Grounds. Random ranged grandite, one story; built early or mid 19th C., moved from Chesterfield, N.H. 2 sheets (1938); 1 ext. photo (1940*), 2 int. photos (1940*).

Eddy, Zachariah, Law Office (MASS-851), Storrowton, Eastern States Exposition Grounds. Frame with clapboarding, one story, segmental roof; built 1810, moved from Eddyville in the town of Middleborough, Mass. 1 ext. photo (1940*).

Gilbert, Levi and Peletiah, House (MASS-850), Storrowton, Eastern States Exposition Grounds. Frame with clapboarding, 2 stories, side wing; built 1794, moved from West Brookfield, Massachusetts. 1 ext. photo (1940*), 3 int. photos (1940*).

Potter, Captain John, House (MASS-852), Storrowton, Eastern States Exposition Grounds. Historic house museum. Frame with clapboarding, brick, two-and-a-half stories, monitor; built c. 1775, moved from North Brookfield, Mass. 9 ext. photos (1940*), 7 int. photos (1940*).

Salisbury Meetinghouse (MASS-843), Storrowton, Eastern States Exposition Grounds. Frame with clapboarding and matched siding, one story with three-stage tower and spire, giant order portico; built 1834 in Salisbury, N.H., dismantled and reconstructed in Storrowton, 1929. 2 int. photos (1940*).

WEST STOCKBRIDGE — *Berkshire County*

Engine House Ruins (MASS-149), near end of Mills St. Fieldstone masonry, one story; built 1838 by Hudson and West Stockbridge Railroad. 1 sheet (1935); 1 ext. photo (1935).

Marble House (MASS-415). Random ashlar, 2 stories; built early 19th C. 1 ext. photo (1935).

Marble Mill (MASS-416). Random ashlar, one story; built early 19th C. 1 ext. photo (1935).

Old Bank Building ("Greek Temple" House) (MASS-496). Frame with clapboarding, two stories, tetrastyle square-columned portico; built early 19th C. 1 ext. photo (1935).

WESTWOOD — *Norfolk County*

Town Pound (MASS-2-32), Grove St. Rectangular fieldstone wall; built 1790. 1 sheet (1934); 1 photo (1934).

WEYMOUTH — *Norfolk County*

Adams, Abigail (Smith), House (MASS-417), 450 Bridge St. Frame with clapboarding, one-and-a-half stories, gambrel roof; built 1740, later alterations and additions. Birthplace of Mrs. John Adams. 1 ext. photo (1941).

First Church (MASS-594). Frame with clapboarding and matched siding, 1 story with pilasters, square two-stage tower with spire; built early 19th C. 1 ext. photo (1941).

Wildes, Captain William, House (MASS-835), 872 Commercial St. Frame with clapboarding, 2 stories, hipped roof and monitor; built 1790. 5 ext. photos (1938), 8 int. photos (1938).

WILLIAMSTOWN — *Berkshire County*

Smedley, Nehimiah, House (MASS-2-18), State Route 2. Frame with clapboarding, 2 stories with overhang; built 1772. 7 sheets (1934); 1 ext. photo (1934), 1 int. photo (1934).

Deming, Titus, House (MASS-106), on road to New Ashford, South Williamstown. Frame with clapboarding, 2 stories; built c. 1800. 6 sheets (1934); 7 ext. photos (1934, 1937).

WILMINGTON — *Middlesex County*

Middlesex Canal Lock-Keeper's House (MASS-380). See Middlesex Canal (MASS-380); Lowell, Mass.

WINTHROP — *Suffolk County*

Winthrop, Deane, House (MASS-575), 40 Shirley Street. Museum. Frame with clapboarding and shingles, two stories, rear lean-to; built c. 1637, later additions and alterations, restored 1908. 2 ext. photos (1941).

WOBURN — *Middlesex County*

Baldwin, Loammi, Mansion (MASS-419), Elm St. Frame with wooden imitation ashlar siding and pilasters, three stories, hipped roof with monitor, rear wing; built c. 1750, later alterations. 9 ext. photos (1936, including outbuildings), 4 int. photos (1936, including outbuildings).

Bartlett, Joseph, House (MASS-276), 827 Main St. Frame with clapboarding and wooden imitation ashlar siding, two stories, hipped roof, two-tiered Doric porch; built 1790–1800, later additions. 7 ext. photos (1936, 1940), 8 int. photos (1940).

Count Rumford House and Garden (MASS-240). See Thompson, Ebenezer, House and Garden (MASS-240); Woburn, Mass.

Horn Pond Tavern (MASS-578). Frame with clapboarding, 2 stories, rear ell; built early 19th C., later additions. 1 ext. photo (1941).

Thompson, Ebenezer, House & Garden (Count Rumford House & Garden) (MASS-240), 90 Elm Street. Frame with clapboarding, two stories, gambrel roof, rear lean-to; house built c. 1700–14, formal garden laid out 1923. The birthplace of Benjamin Thompson (Count Rumford). 2 sheets (1937–38); 4 ext. photos (1940).

WORCESTER — *Worcester County*

Salisbury Mansion No. 2 (MASS-574). Frame with wooden imitation ashlar siding, two-and-a-half stories, hipped roof, Doric porches; built early 19th C. 2 photocopies of photos (1920's or 1930's, including coach house wing).

Salisbury, Stephen, Mansion (MASS-573). Frame with clapboarding, two stories, hipped roof with deck balustrade, Ionic porch; built early 19th C. 1 photocopy of ext. photo (20th C.).

WORTHINGTON — *Hampshire County*

Woodbridge, Jonathan, House (MASS-124), Worthington Corners. Frame with clapboarding, 2 stories, hipped roof; built 1806. 21 sheets (1934).

WRENTHAM — *Norfolk County*

Fisher, David, House (Gray Door Inn) (MASS-420). Frame with clapboarding, two stories; built early 19th C. 2 ext. photos (1936, 1937), 2 int. photos (1937).

140

Guild-Kollock House (MASS-421). Frame with clapboarding, one-and-a-half stories, gambrel roof; built mid 18th C. 3 ext. photos (1936), 6 int. photos (1936).

YARMOUTH — *Barnstable County*

Kelley, Elizabeth, House (MASS-296). Frame with shingles, one-and-a-half stories; built late 18th C. 1 ext. photo (1935), 1 int. photo (1935).

Historic American
Buildings Survey

PHOTOGRAPHS

ACOAXET, Richmond-Manchester House.

ACTON, Faulkner House.

ADAMS, Society of Friends (Quaker) Meetinghouse.

AGAWAM, Colton-Cooley House.

AGAWAM, Captain Charles Leonard House.

AMESBURY, Rocky Hill Meetinghouse.

AMESBURY, Rocky Hill Meetinghouse.

AMHERST, Boltwood-Stockbridge House.

AMHERST, Nehemiah Strong House.

ANDOVER, Benjamin Abbot Farmhouse.

ANNISQUAM, Custom House.

ANNISQUAM, William Hodgkin Tide Mill.

ARLINGTON, Calvary Methodist Episcopal Church Tower.

ARLINGTON, Jason Russell House.

ASHBY, Asa Kendall House.

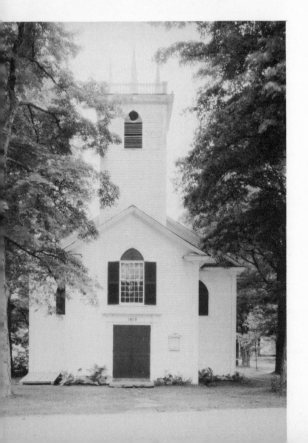

ASHFIELD, St. John's Episcopal Church.

ASHFIELD, Town Hall.

ATTLEBORO, Joel Robinson House.

ATTLEBORO VICINITY, John Daggett House.

AUBURN, Thaddeus Chapin House.

BARNSTABLE, Isaac Gorham House.

BEDFORD, First Parish Unitarian Meetinghouse.

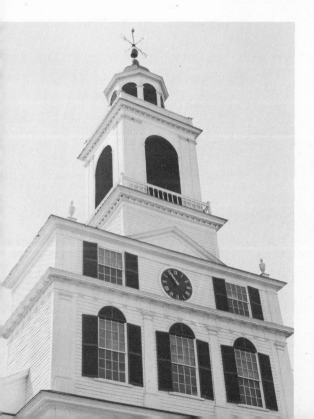

BEDFORD, Penniman-Stearns House.

BEDFORD, Pollard Tavern.

BEVERLY, John Balch House.

BEVERLY, John Cabot House.

BEVERLY, Powder House.

BILLERICA, Allen Tavern.

BILLERICA, Dr. William Bowers House.

BILLERICA, Honorable Joseph Locke House.

BILLERICA VICINITY, Ensign Samuel Manning Manse.

BLACKSTONE, Old Stone Building.

BOSTON, Abolition Church.

BOSTON, Amory-Ticknor House.

BOSTON, Amory-Ticknor House.

BOSTON, Bela and Caleb
Clap House.

BOSTON, Clough-Langdon House.

BOSTON, Clough-Langdon House.

BOSTON, Faneuil Hall.

BOSTON, Faneuil Hall.

BOSTON, Fort Independence.

BOSTON, Fort Independence.

BOSTON, Hollis Street Church.

BOSTON, Hollis Street Theater.

BOSTON, India Wharf Stores.

BOSTON, Marshall-Hancock House.

BOSTON, Massachusetts Charitable Mechanic Association Exhibition Hall.

BOSTON, Massachusetts
Institute of Technology
Rogers Building.

BOSTON, Massachusetts Institute of Technology
Rogers Building.

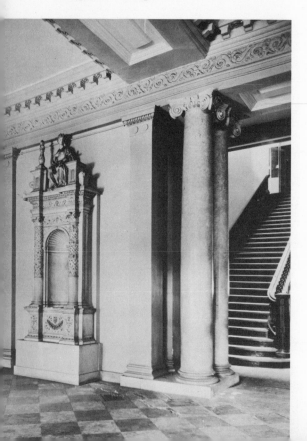

BOSTON, Massachusetts Institute of Technology Rogers Building.

BOSTON, Mayhew School.

BOSTON, Mayhew School.

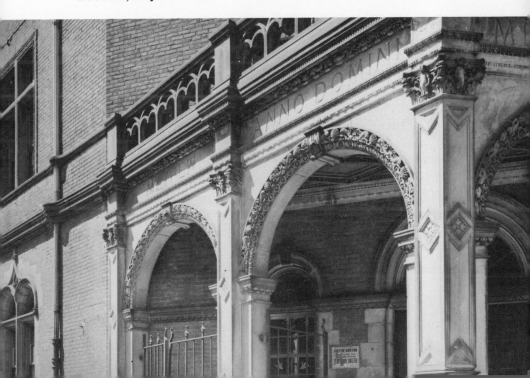

BOSTON, Mayhew School.

BOSTON, Parkman Market.

BOSTON, St. Patrick's
Church.

BOSTON, Toolhouse.

BOSTON VICINITY,
Milestones.

BREWSTER, Stony Brook Mill.

BREWSTER, Winslow House.

BRIDGEWATER, Andrews House.

BRIDGEWATER, Hayward House.

BROOKFIELD, Banister House.

BROOKFIELD, Colonel J. Crosby House.

BUCKLAND, Mary Lyon House.

BUCKLAND, Mary Lyon House.

BURLINGTON, William H.
Winn House.

BURLINGTON, Francis
Wyman House.

BURLINGTON, Francis Wyman House.

CAMBRIDGE, General William Brattle House.

CAMBRIDGE, Christ Church.

CAMBRIDGE, Harvard University, Holden Chapel.

CAMBRIDGE, Harvard University, Hollis Hall.

**CAMBRIDGE, Longfellow
House.**

CARLISLE, Unitarian
Church.

CARVER, Sturtevant House.

CHARLESTOWN, Major
Adams House.

CHARLESTOWN, Andrews-
Getchell House.

CHARLESTOWN, General
Charles Devens House.

CHARLESTOWN, Edward
Everett House.

CHARLESTOWN, 11 Devens Street.

CHARLESTOWN, Hyde-Worthen House.

CHARLTON, General Salem Towne House.

CHATHAM, Joseph Atwood House.

CHATHAM, Joseph Atwood House.

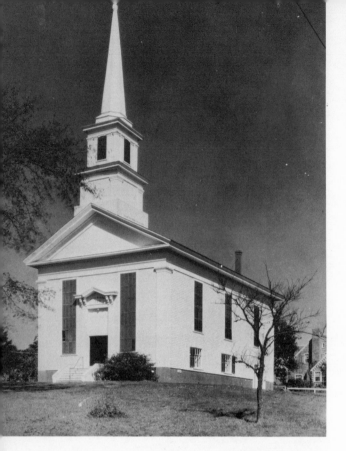

CHATHAM, Congregational Church.

CHATHAM, Captain Solomon Howes House.

CHATHAM PORT, Christopher Ryder House.

WEST CHATHAM, Buck House.

CHELMSFORD, Fiske House.

CHELSEA, Captains' Row.

CHELSEA, Captains' Row.

CHELSEA, Cary-Bellingham Mansion.

CHELSEA, Bevis Tucker ("Octagon") House.

CHESTER, Reverend Aaron Bascom House.

CLARKSBURG, Musterfield House.

COHASSET, Cushing-Nichols House.

COHASSET, Fitch House.

COHASSET, Reverend Nehemiah Hobart House.

CONCORD, Jones-Keyes House.

CONCORD, Old Bank Building.

CONCORD, "Old Manse."

CONCORD, "Orchard House."

CONCORD, "The Wayside."

CONCORD, Wright Tavern.

CONWAY, Joe Herrick House.

DANVERS, Judge Samuel Holton House.

DANVERS, Rebecca Nurse House.

DANVERS, Elias Endicott Porter House.

DANVERS, General Israel Putnam House.

DARTMOUTH, Apponagansett Meetinghouse.

DARTMOUTH, Apponagansett Meetinghouse.

DEDHAM, Jonathan Fairbanks House.

DEDHAM, Fisher-Whiting House.

DEDHAM, Samuel Haven House.

DEDHAM, Powder House.

DEERFIELD VILLAGE, Captain Thomas Dickinson
House.

DEERFIELD VILLAGE,
David Dickinson House.

DEERFIELD VILLAGE, First Church of Deerfield.

DEERFIELD VILLAGE, Frary-Barnard House.

DEERFIELD VILLAGE, Memorial Hall (First Deer-field Academy).

DEERFIELD VILLAGE, Godfrey Nims House.

DEERFIELD VILLAGE, Joseph Stebbins House.

DEERFIELD VILLAGE, Wells-Thorn House.

DEERFIELD VILLAGE, Parson John Williams
House.

DEERFIELD VILLAGE VICINITY, Allen House—
Fuller Studio.

DEERFIELD VILLAGE VICINITY, Wapping School.

DIGHTON, Coram House.

DIGHTON, Delare Cottage.

NORTH DIGHTON, Captain
John Clouston House.

DORCHESTER, Bird-Sawyer House.

DORCHESTER, James Blake House.

**DORCHESTER, First Parish
Unitarian Church.**

**DORCHESTER, Lyceum
Hall.**

DORCHESTER, Thomas Pierce House.

DOVER, Caryl Parsonage.

DOVER, Chickering House.

DOVER, First Parish Meetinghouse.

DUXBURY, "King" Caesar House.

EGREMONT, Town Hall.

FAIRHAVEN, Old Academy.

FAIRHAVEN, Old Academy.

FALL RIVER, Richard Borden Manufacturing Company No. 1 Mill.

FALL RIVER, Richard Borden Manufacturing Company No. 1 Mill.

FALL RIVER, Durfee Mills.

FALL RIVER, Durfee Mills.

FALL RIVER, Durfee Mills.

FALL RIVER, Metacomet Mill.

FALL RIVER, Metacomet Mill.

FALL RIVER, Union Mills.

FALL RIVER, Union Mills.

FRAMINGHAM, Jonathan Eames House.

FRAMINGHAM, First Baptist Church.

FRAMINGHAM, Framingham Academy.

FRAMINGHAM, Gates House.

FRAMINGHAM,   Kellogg
House.

FRAMINGHAM, Pike-Haven–Foster House.

FRAMINGHAM VICINITY, Howe-Gregory House.

GEORGETOWN, 36 East Main Street.

GILL, Red House.

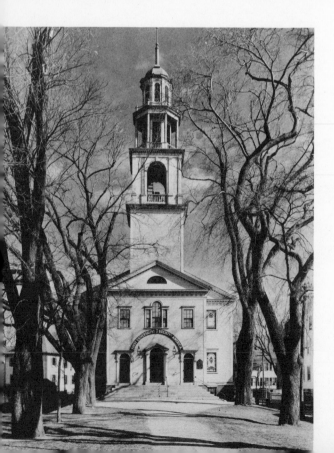

GLOUCESTER, First Universalist Church.

GLOUCESTER, First Universalist Church.

GLOUCESTER, First Universalist Church.

GREAT BARRINGTON, General Joseph Dwight House.

GREENFIELD, Coleman-Hollister House.

GREENFIELD, Gould-Potter House.

GREENFIELD, Leavitt-Hovey House.

GREENFIELD, Reverend
Roger Newton House.

GREENFIELD VICINITY,
McHard House.

GROTON, Andrew Robbins House.

HADLEY, Huntington House.

HADLEY, Samuel Porter House.

HADLEY, Colonel Ruggles Woodbridge House.

HADLEY, Colonel Ruggles
Woodbridge House.

HADLEY, Wright House.

HALIFAX, Shadrach Standish House.

HALIFAX, Shadrach Standish House.

HALIFAX, Timothy Wood House.

HAMILTON-IPSWICH, Warner's Bridge.

HATFIELD, Cornelia Bil-
lings House.

HATFIELD, Lieutenant David Billings House.

HATFIELD, Lieutenant David Billings House.

HATFIELD, Morton House.

HAVERHILL, Thomas Dustin House.

HINGHAM, John Beal House.

HINGHAM, Cushing House.

HINGHAM, General Benjamin Lincoln House.

HINGHAM, Perez Lincoln House.

HINGHAM, Thomas Loring House.

HINGHAM, Daniel Shute House.

HINGHAM, Jabez Wilder House.

HINGHAM, Jabez Wilder House.

IPSWICH, Choate Bridge.

IPSWICH, John Heard House.

IPSWICH, 40 North Main Street.

IPSWICH, Howard Emerson House.

IPSWICH, John Kimball House.

IPSWICH, Norton-Corbett House.

IPSWICH, Old Post Office.

IPSWICH, Proctor House.

IPSWICH, Treadwell House.

IPSWICH, Colonel Nathaniel Wade House.

JAMAICA PLAIN, Loring-Greenough House.

KINGSTON, Major John Bradford House.

KINGSTON, Major John Bradford House.

KINGSTON, Major John Bradford House.

KINGSTON, Holmes House.

KINGSTON, Holmes House.

KINGSTON, Squire William Sever House.

KINGSTON, Squire William Sever House.

KINGSTON, Captain Thomas Willett House.

LAKEVILLE, Jennie Sampson House.

LAKEVILLE, Jennie Sampson House.

LAKEVILLE, Jennie Samp-son House.

LAKEVILLE, George Ward House.

LANESBOROUGH, Registry of Deeds Building.

LEXINGTON, Buckman Tavern.

LEXINGTON, Hancock-Clarke House.

LEXINGTON, Jonathan Harrington Jr. House.

LEXINGTON, Munroe Tavern.

LEXINGTON, Stone Building.

LONGMEADOW, Captain Gideon Colton House.

LONGMEADOW, Colonel Alexander Field House.

LOWELL, James Abbott McNeill Whistler's Birthplace.

MANCHESTER, Major Israel Forster House.

MANCHESTER, Orthodox
Congregational Church.

MANCHESTER, Orthodox
Congregational Church.

MARBLEHEAD, Robert "King" Hooper House.

MARBLEHEAD, Robert "King" Hooper House.

**MARBLEHEAD, Peter
Jayne House.**

**MARBLEHEAD, Peter
Jayne House.**

MARBLEHEAD, Old Gun (Artillery) House.

MARBLEHEAD, Powder House.

MARBLEHEAD, Town House.

MARBLEHEAD, Captain Samuel Trevett House.

MARBLEHEAD, William Waters House and Bakery.

MARSHFIELD, Walter Hatch House.

MARSHFIELD, Walter Hatch House.

MARSHFIELD, Anthony Thomas House.

MARSHFIELD, George H. Weatherbee House.

MARSHFIELD, Winslow House.

MARSHFIELD HILLS, Nathaniel Clift House.

MEDFIELD, Seth Clark ("Peak") House.

MEDFIELD, Seth Clark ("Peak") House.

MEDFORD, Andrew Hall House.

MEDFORD, Thatcher Magoun House.

MEDFORD, Reverend David Osgood House.

MEDFORD, Usher-Royall House.

MEDFORD,   Usher-Royall House.

MEDFORD,   Usher-Royall House.

**MEDFORD,   Usher-Royall
House Slave Quarters.**

**MEDFORD,   Usher-Royall
House Slave Quarters.**

MELROSE, Ensign Thomas Lynde House.

MELROSE, Phineas Upham House.

MIDDLEBOROUGH, Central Methodist Church.

MIDDLEBOROUGH, First Congregational Church Carriage Sheds.

MIDDLEBOROUGH, Mill Houses.

MIDDLEBOROUGH, Old Tavern Inn.

MIDDLEBOROUGH, Colonel P. H. Peirce Store.

MIDDLEBOROUGH, E. Robinson Store.

MIDDLEBOROUGH, Deborah Sampson House.

MIDDLEBOROUGH, Sproat House.

MIDDLEBOROUGH, Venus Thompson House.

MIDDLEBOROUGH, Silas Wood House.

MIDDLETOWN, Bradstreet House.

MILLVILLE, Covered Bridge.

MILLVILLE VICINITY, Chestnut Hill Meeting-house.

MILLVILLE VICINITY, Chestnut Hill Meeting-house.

MILTON, Governor Jonathan Belcher House.

MILTON, Governor Jonathan Belcher Summer House.

MILTON, Isaac Davenport House.

MILTON, Joseph N. Howe House.

MILTON, Powder House.

MONTAGUE, Covered Bridge.

NANTUCKET, John Wendell Barrett House.

NANTUCKET, Reuben R. Bunker House.

NANTUCKET, Henry Coffin House.

NANTUCKET, Jared Coffin House.

NANTUCKET, Jethro Coffin House.

NANTUCKET, Joshua Coffin House.

NANTUCKET, Major Josiah Coffin House.

NANTUCKET, Coffin-Athearn Stores.

NANTUCKET, Coffin-Gardner House.

NANTUCKET, Elihu Coleman House.

NANTUCKET, First Congregational Church.

NANTUCKET, First Congregational Church.

**NANTUCKET, First
Congregational Church.**

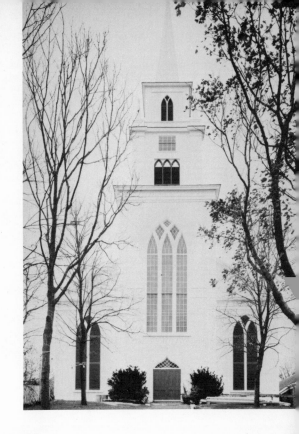

**NANTUCKET, India Street
Neighborhood Study.**

NANTUCKET, Nantucket Athenaeum.

NANTUCKET, Orange and Union Streets Neighborhood Study.

NANTUCKET, Orange and Union Streets Neighborhood Study, Levi Starbuck House.

NANTUCKET, William Rotch Building.

NANTUCKET, William Rotch Building.

NANTUCKET, Second Congregational Meeting-house.

**NANTUCKET, Joseph Star-
buck Houses.**

**NANTUCKET, Thomas
Starbuck Homestead.**

NATICK, Henry Wilson Shoe Shop.

NEW BEDFORD, Custom House.

NEW BEDFORD, Friends
Meetinghouse.

NEW BEDFORD, Joseph Grinnell Mansion.

NEW BEDFORD, Institution for Savings.

NEW BEDFORD, Merchants' and Mechanics' Banks Building.

NEW BEDFORD, William R. Rodman House.

NEW BEDFORD, William J. Rotch House.

NEW BEDFORD, William J.
Rotch House.

NEW BEDFORD, William J.
Rotch House.

NEW BEDFORD, Henry Taber House.

NEW BEDFORD, William Tallman Warehouse.

NEW BEDFORD, Wamsutta Mill.

NEW BEDFORD, Ware-
house.

NEWBURY, Tristram Coffin House.

NEWBURY, Richard Jackman House.

NEWBURY, Short House.

NEWBURY, Swett-Ilsley House.

NEWBURY, Dr. Peter Toppan House.

NEWBURYPORT, John N. Cushing House.

NEWBURYPORT, Gaol and Gaoler's House.

NEWBURYPORT, Gaol and Gaoler's Barn.

NEWBURYPORT, Globe Steam Mills.

NEWBURYPORT, Hennesey House.

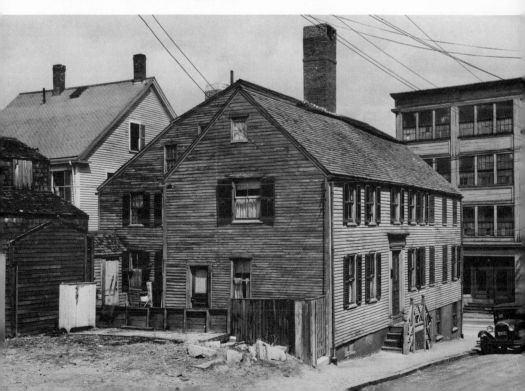

NEWBURYPORT, Highway Cut-off Demolition.

NEWBURYPORT, Highway Cut-off Demolition.

NEWBURYPORT, Highway Cut-off Demolition.

NEWBURYPORT, Marden House.

NEWBURYPORT, Meeting-house of First Religious Society.

NEWBURYPORT, Joseph Moulton House.

NEWBURYPORT, Benjamin Pierce House.

NEWBURYPORT, Regan House.

NEWBURYPORT, Charles Stockman House.

NEWBURYPORT, Thibault House.

NEWBURYPORT, Thurlow House.

NEWBURYPORT, Abraham Wheelwright House.

NEWTON, Timothy Jackson House.

NEWTON, Kendrick House.

NEWTON, Mill Houses.

NEWTON, Mill Houses.

NEWTON, Mill Houses.

NEWTON, St. Mary's Epis-
copal Church.

NEWTON, John Woodward House.

NEWTON, Wyman-Tower House.

NORTHAMPTON, Isaac Damon House.

NORTHAMPTON, Isaac
Damon House.

NORTHAMPTON, Isaac Damon House.

NORTHAMPTON, Allen House.

NORTH ANDOVER, Governor Simon Bradstreet House.

NORTH ANDOVER, Dr. Thomas Kittredge House.

NORTH ATTLEBOROUGH,
Handel Daggett House.

NORTH ATTLEBOROUGH,
Jabez Ellis House.

NORTH ATTLEBOROUGH, Dr. Bezaleel Mann
House.

NORTH ATTLEBOROUGH,
Dr. Bezaleel Mann House.

NORTH ATTLEBOROUGH VICINITY, Stanley-Mathewson House.

NORTH ATTLEBOROUGH VICINITY, Stanley-Mathewson House.

NORTHFIELD, Hall-Spring House.

NORTHFIELD, Captain Samuel Lane House.

NORTHFIELD, Isaac Mattoon House.

NORTHFIELD, William Pomeroy House.

NORTHFIELD, White-Field House.

NORTHFIELD VICINITY, Simeon Alexander House.

NORTHFIELD VICINITY, Elijah E. Belding House.

NORTHFIELD VICINITY, Captain Richard Colton House.

NORTH READING, Guy M. Crosby Jr. House.

NORTH READING, Guy M. Crosby Jr. House.

NORTON, Jonathan Newcomb House.

NORWELL, Bryant-Cushing House.

NORWELL, Bryant-Cushing House.

NORWELL, Bryant-Cushing House.

OAKHAM, Eli Adams House.

OAKHAM, Old Saw Mill.

ORLEANS, Jonathan Kendrick House.

PEPPERELL, Colonel William Prescott House.

PITTSFIELD, "Arrowhead" (Bush-Melville House).

PITTSFIELD, Bulfinch
Church.

PITTSFIELD, Bulfinch
Church.

PLAINVILLE, Benjamin Slack House.

PRESCOTT, Red School House.

QUINCY, John Quincy Adams' Birthplace.

QUINCY, Adams Mansion.

QUINCY, Colonel Josiah Quincy House.

QUINCY, Colonel Josiah Quincy House.

QUINCY, Colonel Josiah Quincy House.

QUINCY, Stone Temple.

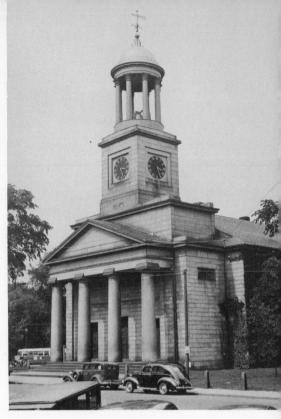

RICHMOND, Peirson House.

ROWLEY, Billings House and Fence.

ROXBURY, Dillaway-Thomas House.

ROXBURY, First Church in Roxbury.

ROXBURY, Edward Everett Hale House.

ROXBURY, Judge Hayden House.

ROXBURY, "Old Puddingstone" Building.

RUTLAND, General Rufus
Putnam House.

SALEM, John Andrew House.

SALEM, Cook-Oliver House.

SALEM, Cook-Oliver House.

SALEM, Crowninshield-Devereux House.

SALEM, Crowninshield Warehouse.

SALEM, Stephen Daniel House.

SALEM, Richard Derby House.

SALEM, Pickering Dodge House.

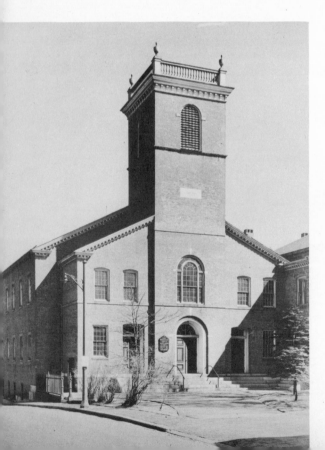

SALEM, First Universalist Meetinghouse.

SALEM, First Universalist
Meetinghouse.

SALEM, Forrester-Peabody House.

SALEM, Gardner-White-Pingree House.

SALEM, Hamilton Hall.

SALEM, General Benjamin Hawkes House.

SALEM, Nathaniel Hawthorne's Birthplace.

SALEM, Loring-Emmerton House.

SALEM, Oliver Primary School.

SALEM, Phillips House.

SALEM, Doctor Phippen House.

SALEM, Jerathmeel Pierce House.

SALEM, Jerathmeel Pierce House.

SALEM, Ropes Memorial.

SALEM, Joshua Ward House.

SALEM, Joshua Ward
House.

SAUGUS, "Scotch" Boardman House.

SCITUATE, "Old Oaken Bucket" House.

SEEKONK, Lieutenant-Governor Simeon Martin House.

SEEKONK, Lieutenant-Governor Simeon Martin House.

SEEKONK, Lieutenant-Governor Simeon Martin House.

SHARON, Cobb's Tavern.

SHEFFIELD, Colonel John Ashley House.

SHEFFIELD, Parker L. Hall Law Office.

SHELBURNE, Arms House.

SHELBURNE, Arms House.

SOMERSET, Jarathmael Bowers House.

SOMERSET, Jarathmael Bowers House.

SOMERSET, John Brayton Homestead.

SOMERSET, Henry Pettis House.

SOMERVILLE, Powder House.

SOMERVILLE, Round Barn.

SOMERVILLE, Round Barn.

SOMERVILLE, Francis Tufts House.

SOMERVILLE, Oliver Tufts House.

SPRINGFIELD, Alexander House.

SPRINGFIELD, Alexander House.

STOCKBRIDGE, Yale-
Duryea Water Mills.

STOCKBRIDGE, Yale-Duryea Water Mills.

STOCKBRIDGE, Yale-
Duryea Water Mills.

STONEHAM, Jonathan Green House.

STOUGHTON, Samuel Atherton House.

STOUGHTON, Washington Hotel,

STURBRIDGE, Oliver Wight House.

SWAMPSCOTT, John Humphrey House.

SWANSEA, Joseph G.
Luther Store.

TAUNTON, EAST, Nathan
Dean House, Privy.

**TAUNTON, EAST, Nathan
Dean House.**

**TOPSFIELD, Parson Joseph
Capen House.**

TOPSFIELD, Elmwood Mansion.

TOWNSEND, Conant House.

TOWNSEND, Spaulding Grist Mill.

TYNGSBOROUGH, Tyng House.

UXBRIDGE, Lieutenant Simeon Wheelock House.

UXBRIDGE, Lieutenant Simeon Wheelock House.

UXBRIDGE, NORTH,
Crown and Eagle Mills.

WAKEFIELD, Colonel James Hartshorne House.

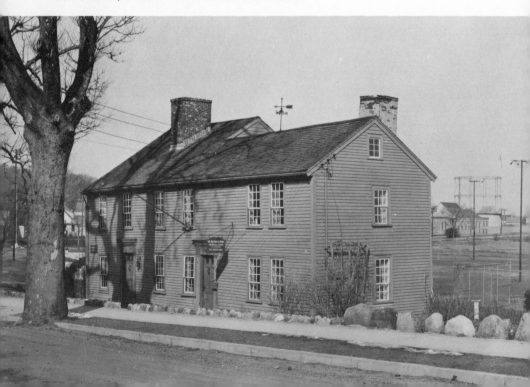

WALTHAM, Stone Mill.

WAREHAM, Israel Fearing House.

WATERTOWN, John Bemis House.

WATERTOWN, Abraham Brown House.

WATERTOWN, Daniel Caldwell House.

WATERTOWN, Conant House.

WAYLAND, Town Bridge.

WELLESLEY, Ellis Stone Barn.

WESTFIELD, Arnold House.

WESTHAMPTON, Captain Jared Hunt House.

WESTON, Golden Ball Tavern.

WESTON, Lamson House.

WESTON, Lawyer's Office.

WESTPORT, Waite-Potter House.

WEST STOCKBRIDGE, Marble House.

WEYMOUTH, Abigail (Smith) Adams House.

WILLIAMSTOWN, Nehimiah Smedley House.

WILLIAMSTOWN, SOUTH, Titus Deming House.

WILLIAMSTOWN, SOUTH, Titus Deming House.

WINTHROP, Deane Winthrop House.

WINTHROP, Deane Winthrop House.

WOBURN, Loammi Baldwin Mansion.

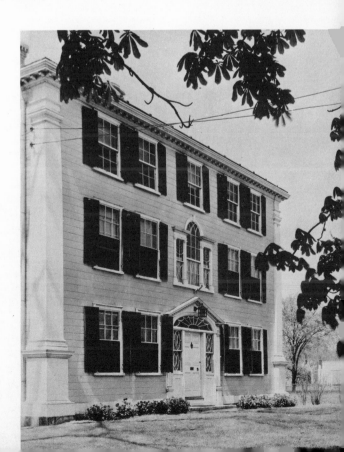

WOBURN, Loammi Baldwin
Mansion.

WOBURN, Joseph Bartlett House.

WOBURN, Count Rumford House.

WORCESTER, Stephen Salisbury Mansion.

WORCESTER, Salisbury Mansion No. 2.

WRENTHAM, David Fisher House.

WRENTHAM, Guild-Kollock House.

YARMOUTH, Elizabeth Kelley House.